Principles of Cost Accounting

Principles of Cost Accounting

Keith Hagar

Clanrye International
www.clanryeinternational.com

Clanrye International,
750 Third Avenue, 9th Floor,
New York, NY 10017, USA

ISBN: 978-1-64726-073-6

Cataloging-in-Publication Data

Principles of cost accounting / Keith Hagar.
p. cm.
Includes bibliographical references and index.
ISBN 978-1-64726-073-6
1. Cost accounting. 2. Accounting. I. Hagar, Keith.
HF5686.C8 P75 2021
657.42--dc23

For information on all Clanrye International publications
visit our website at www.clanryeinternational.com

CLANRYE
INTERNATIONAL

Contents

Preface

Cost accounting refers to the group of procedures used to record and report measurements of the cost of manufacturing goods and services in detail. There are various cost accounting approaches including activity-based costing, environmental accounting, project accounting, resource consumption accounting, standard cost accounting and life cycle costing. Cost accounting provides the management with the detailed cost information for controlling current operations and planning for the future. It enables the optimization of the business processes and practices on the basis of capability and cost efficiency. The fundamental elements of this field are materials, labor and expenses. Materials are broadly divided into direct and indirect materials on the basis of their cost and visibility in the final product. This book elucidates the concepts and innovative models around prospective developments with respect to cost accounting. It picks up individual branches and explains their needs and contribution in the context of a growing economy. This book will provide comprehensive knowledge to the readers.

Given below is the chapter wise description of the book:

Chapter 1- The processing, measurement and communication of non-financial and financial information regarding economic entities is known as accounting. This is an introductory chapter which will provide a brief introduction of all the significant aspects of accounting such as accounting principles, accounting standard and accounting system.

Chapter 2- The value of money which has been spent to produce something or to deliver a service is known as its cost. The set of procedures for the purpose of recording and reporting measurements of the cost incurred in manufacturing goods and providing services is known as cost accounting. The topics elaborated in this chapter will help in gaining a better perspective about cost accounting as well as its purpose and importance.

Chapter 3- Some of the fundamental concepts and elements of cost accounting are cost principle, cost allocation, variable cost, fixed cost, short-run cost, long-run cost, labor and overheads. The chapter closely examines these key concepts of cost accounting to provide an extensive understanding of the subject.

Chapter 4- Costs are broadly divided into a number of categories such as average cost, direct cost and indirect cost. Average cost is further subdivided into average fixed cost and average variable cost. All the diverse aspects of these types of cost have been carefully analyzed in this chapter.

Chapter 5- There are a number of different methods and types of cost accounting. Some of them are activity-based costing, standard cost accounting, marginal costing, lean accounting and target costing. These topics have been carefully elaborated in this chapter to provide a holistic understanding of the subject.

Chapter 6- There are a number of different tools which are used for managing cost such as capital budgeting, cost variability, capacity management and inventory valuation. The chapter closely examines these key methods of managing cost as well as details the different types of capital budgeting to provide an extensive understanding of the subject.

Chapter 7- The framework which is used by companies for estimating the cost of their products for the purpose of analyzing the profitability, cost control and inventory valuation is known as cost accounting system. This chapter has been carefully written to provide an easy understanding of the varied facets of cost accounting systems as well as their types, advantages and disadvantages.

At the end, I would like to thank all those who dedicated their time and efforts for the successful completion of this book. I also wish to convey my gratitude towards my friends and family who supported me at every step.

Keith Hagar

1

Basics of Accounting

The processing, measurement and communication of non-financial and financial information regarding economic entities is known as accounting. This is an introductory chapter which will provide a brief introduction of all the significant aspects of accounting such as accounting principles, accounting standard and accounting system.

Accounting involves the systematic process of recording, summarizing, analyzing, and reporting financial information, including the profit and loss for a given time period and a company's assets and liabilities. Part of the process of accounting includes reporting financial information to third parties, such as tax collectors. Accounting is one of the core departments at any organization, as businesses rely on financial information to make decisions and develop strategies, and it is carried out by accountants and bookkeepers. It could also be part of a larger finance department.

In general, more complex accounting transactions are made by Certified Public Accountants (CPAs). When producing financial statements, accountants use what are called Generally Accepted Accounting Principles (GAAP), including what is called double-entry accounting, in which each expense or credit is entered in two places on a company's balance sheet. The sheets are then reconciled with each other in a process called balancing the books.

Basic Accounting Terms

Assets

Assets are the wealth that has been accumulated by the business and is owned outright without lien or loan. It may be items that depreciate over time, or goods that are sold to customers. This may include cash and investments, buildings and property, accounts receivable, warehouse inventory, equipment and supplies.

Balance Sheet

The balance sheet is an important aspect of business. It records the basic accounting formula of assets = liabilities + stockholder equity / capital at a certain point in time, either monthly, quarterly or yearly. From the balance sheet the financial health of the business can be ascertained.

General Ledger

The general ledger is the side of the bookkeeping ledger that contains the balance sheet and the income statement accounts. Here all business transactions are recorded, including sales, credit purchases, office expenses and income losses.

Margin

Gross margin or profit is the total number of sales that have been made, subtracted by the associated costs, such as manufacturing costs, wholesales costs, material, and supplies.

Loss

When a service or product sells for less than what it cost to supply or manufacture it, or when expenses have exceeded revenues of a particular asset, it's called a loss.

On Credit/On Account

On credit or on account means that products or services have been sold with the use of credit. Payment has not immediately been provided for these items, and there may be terms on account that may result in interest charges.

Receipts

Receipts is the total amount of cash collected in business transactions over the course of one day. It does not include other revenue collected.

Revenue

Income and revenue are interchangeable, compromising the total amount of all income collected at one point in time. It may include cash sales, credit purchases, subscription fees and interest income. It differs from receipts, as it can include monies that are not collected at the delivery time.

Trade Discount

A trade discount is a percentage discounted from the purchase price, and is based on the volume of goods ordered at one point in time. Higher discounts may be applicable to larger orders, with smaller discounts for lesser orders.

Trial Balance

The trial balance is recorded in the general ledger, and includes both debits and credits for one particular account. The sheet must balance, with debits equaling credits.

Elements of Basic Accounting

Assets

Assets refer to resources owned and controlled by the entity as a result of past transactions and events, from which future economic benefits are expected to flow to the entity. In simple terms, assets are *properties or rights owned by the business.* They may be classified as current or non-current.

(a) Current assets – Assets are considered current if they are held for the purpose of being traded, expected to be realized or consumed within twelve months after the end of the period or its normal operating cycle (whichever is longer), or if it is cash. Examples of current asset accounts are:

1. Cash and Cash Equivalents – bills, coins, funds for current purposes, checks, cash in bank, etc.
2. Receivables – Accounts Receivable (receivable from customers), Notes Receivable (receivables supported by promissory notes), Rent Receivable, Interest Receivable, Due from Employees (or Advances to Employees), and other claims.
    - Allowance for Doubtful Accounts – This is a valuation account which shows the estimated uncollectible amount of accounts receivable. It is a contra-asset account and is presented as a deduction to the related asset – accounts receivable.
3. Inventories – assets held *for sale* in the ordinary course of business.
4. Prepaid expenses – expenses paid in advance, such as, Prepaid Rent, Prepaid Insurance, Prepaid Advertising, and Office Supplies.

(b) Non-current assets – Assets that do not meet the criteria to be classified as current. Hence, they are long-term in nature – useful for a period longer that 12 months or the company's normal operating cycle. Examples of non-current asset accounts include:

1. Long-term investments – investments for long-term purposes such as investment in stocks, bonds, and properties; and funds set up for long-term purposes.
2. Land – land area owned for business operations (not for sale).
3. Building – such as office building, factory, warehouse, or store.
4. Equipment – Machinery, Furniture and Fixtures (shelves, tables, chairs, etc.), Office Equipment, Computer Equipment, Delivery Equipment, and others:
    - Accumulated Depreciation – This is a valuation account which represents the decrease in value of a fixed asset due to continued use, wear & tear,

passage of time, and obsolescence. It is a contra-asset account and is presented as a deduction to the related fixed asset.

5. Intangibles – long-term assets with no physical substance, such as goodwill, patent, copyright, trademark, etc.

6. Other long-term assets.

Liabilities

Liabilities are *economic obligations* or *payables* of the business.

Company assets come from 2 major sources – borrowings from lenders or creditors, and contributions by the owners. The first refers to liabilities; the second to capital.

Liabilities represent claims by other parties aside from the owners against the assets of a company.

Like assets, liabilities may be classified as either current or non-current.

(a) Current liabilities – A liability is considered current if it is due within 12 months after the end of the balance sheet date. In other words, they are expected to be paid in the next year.

If the company's normal operating cycle is longer than 12 months, a liability is considered current if it is due within the operating cycle.

Current liabilities include:

1. Trade and other payables – such as Accounts Payable, Notes Payable, Interest Payable, Rent Payable, Accrued Expenses, etc.

2. Current provisions – estimated short-term liabilities that are probable and can be measured reliably.

3. Short-term borrowings – financing arrangements, credit arrangements or loans that are short-term in nature.

4. Current-portion of a long-term liability – the portion of a long-term borrowing that is currently due:

    - For long-term loans that are to be paid in annual installments, the *portion* to be paid next year is considered current liability; the rest, non-current.

5. Current tax liabilities – taxes for the period and are currently payable.

(b) Non-current liabilities – Liabilities are considered non-current if they are not currently payable, i.e. they are not due within the next 12 months after the end of the accounting period or the company's normal operating cycle, whichever is shorter.

In other words, non-current liabilities are those that do not meet the criteria to be considered current. Hah! Make sense? Non-current liabilities include:

1. Long-term notes, bonds, and mortgage payables;
2. Deferred tax liabilities; and
3. Other long-term obligations.

Capital

Also known as net assets or equity, capital refers to what is left to the owners after all liabilities are settled. Simply stated, capital is equal to total assets minus total liabilities. Capital is affected by the following:

1. Initial and additional contributions of owner/s (investments),
2. Withdrawals made by owner/s (dividends for corporations),
3. Income, and
4. Expenses.

Owner contributions and income increase capital. Withdrawals and expenses decrease it.

The terms used to refer to a company's capital portion varies according to the form of ownership. In a sole proprietorship business, the capital is called Owner's Equity or Owner's Capital; in partnerships, it is called Partners' Equity or Partners' Capital; and in corporations, Stockholders' Equity.

In addition to the three elements mentioned above, there are two items that are also considered as key elements in accounting. They are income and expense. Nonetheless, these items are ultimately included as part of capital.

Income

Income refers to an increase in economic benefit during the accounting period in the form of an increase in asset or a decrease in liability that results in increase in equity, other than contribution from owners.

Income encompasses revenues and gains:

1. Revenues refer to the amounts earned from the company's ordinary course of business such as professional fees or service revenue for service companies and sales for merchandising and manufacturing concerns.
2. Gains come from other activities, such as gain on sale of equipment, gain on sale of short-term investments, and other gains.

Income is measured every period and is ultimately included in the capital account. Examples of income accounts are: Service Revenue, Professional Fees, Rent Income, Commission Income, Interest Income, Royalty Income, and Sales.

Expense

Expenses are decreases in economic benefit during the accounting period in the form of a decrease in asset or an increase in liability that result in decrease in equity, other than distribution to owners.

Expenses include *ordinary expenses* such as Cost of Sales, Advertising Expense, Rent Expense, Salaries Expense, Income Tax, Repairs Expense, etc.; and *losses* such as Loss from Fire, Typhoon Loss, and Loss from Theft. Like income, expenses are also measured every period and then closed as part of capital.

Net income refers to all income minus all expenses.

Process of Accounting

A sequence of activities involving the recording of how cash is received and paid out in a company or organization. The accounting process in business is based on four accounting methods, which are: the accrual method, the consistency method, the prudence method and the going concern method.

Steps involved in Accounting Process

Identifying and Analyzing Business Transactions

The accounting process starts with identifying and analyzing business transactions and events. Not all transactions and events are entered into the accounting system. Only those that pertain to the business entity are included in the process.

For example, a personal loan made by the owner that does not have anything to do with the business entity is not accounted for.

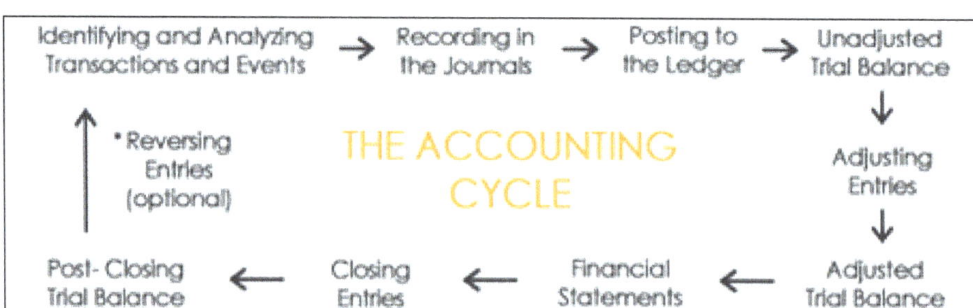

The transactions identified are then analyzed to determine the accounts affected and the amounts to be recorded.

The first step includes the preparation of business documents, or *source documents*. A business document serves as basis for recording a transaction.

Recording in the Journals

A journal is a book – paper or electronic – in which transactions are recorded. Business transactions are recorded using the double-entry bookkeeping system. They are recorded in journal entries containing at least two accounts (one debited and one credited).

To simplify the recording process, special journals are often used for transactions that recur frequently such as sales, purchases, cash receipts, and cash disbursements. A general journal is used to record those that cannot be entered in the special books.

Transactions are recorded in chronological order and as they occur.

Journals are also known as Books of Original Entry.

Posting to the Ledger

Also known as *Books of Final Entry*, the ledger is a collection of accounts that shows the changes made to each account as a result of past transactions, and their current balances.

After the posting all transactions to the ledger, the balances of each account can now be determined.

For example, all journal entry debits and credits made to Cash would be transferred into the Cash account in the ledger. We will be able to calculate the increases and decreases in cash; thus, the ending balance of Cash can be determined.

Unadjusted Trial Balance

A trial balance is prepared to test the equality of the debits and credits. All account balances are extracted from the ledger and arranged in one report. Afterwards, all debit balances are added. All credit balances are also added. Total debits should be equal to total credits.

When errors are discovered, *correcting entries* are made to rectify them or reverse their effect. Take note however that the purpose of a trial balance is only test the equality of total debits and total credits and not to determine the correctness of accounting records.

Some errors could exist even if debits are equal to credits, such as double posting or failure to record a transaction.

Adjusting Entries

Adjusting entries are prepared as an application of the accrual basis of accounting. At the end of the accounting period, some expenses may have been incurred but not yet recorded in the journals. Some income may have been earned but not entered in the books.

Adjusting entries are prepared to update the accounts before they are summarized in the financial statements.

Adjusting entries are made for accrual of income, accrual of expenses, deferrals (income method or liability method), prepayments (asset method or expense method), depreciation, and allowances.

Adjusted Trial Balance

An *adjusted trial balance* may be prepared after adjusting entries are made and before the financial statements are prepared. This is to test if the debits are equal to credits after adjusting entries are made.

Financial Statements

When the accounts are already up-to-date and equality between the debits and credits have been tested, the financial statements can now be prepared. The financial statements are the end-products of an accounting system.

A complete set of financial statements is made up of: (1) Statement of Comprehensive Income *(Income Statement and Other Comprehensive Income),* (2) Statement of Changes in Equity, (3) Statement of Financial Position or *Balance Sheet,* (4) Statement of Cash Flows, and (5) Notes to Financial Statements.

Closing Entries

Temporary or nominal accounts, i.e. income statement accounts, are closed to prepare the system for the next accounting period. Temporary accounts include *income, expense, and withdrawal* accounts. These items are measured periodically.

The accounts are closed to a summary account (usually, Income Summary) and then closed further to the appropriate capital account. Take note that closing entries are made only for temporary accounts. Real or permanent accounts, i.e. balance sheet accounts, are not closed.

Post-closing Trial Balance

In the accounting cycle, the last step is to prepare a post-closing trial balance. It is prepared to test the equality of debits and credits after closing entries are made. Since temporary accounts are already closed at this point, the post-closing trial balance contains real accounts only.

Reversing Entries

Optional step at the *beginning* of the new accounting period:

- Reversing entries are optional: They are prepared at the beginning of the new accounting period to facilitate a smoother and more consistent recording process.
- In this step, the *adjusting entries* made for accrual of income, accrual of expenses, deferrals under the income method, and prepayments under the expense method are simply reversed.

Accounting Principles

Economic Entity Assumption

Ever wonder why your accountant harps on you about keeping your business transactions separate from your personal transactions? This isn't because your business accountant wants to make their job easier (although, yes, separate transactions definitely do help!).

The reason they won't budge on this? The economic entity assumption principle. It basically means that a business is an entity unto itself, and should be treated as such (which is also why this is sometimes called the "separate entity assumption"). If you know this basic accounting principle definition, you'll better under the reason why your accountant insisted you open a separate business bank account when you opened your business. This is business 101.

Even in a sole proprietorship, where your business activity appears on your personal tax return, the economic entity assumption still applies. This is because, legally, your business can exist independently of you. And, another plus is that this will make your life easier if you ever decide to incorporate down the road.

Monetary Unit Assumption

The monetary unit assumption principle dictates all activity be recorded in the same currency. This is why you have to go through the extra effort to complete your business bookkeeping for foreign transactions.

Another assumption under this basic accounting principle is that the purchasing power of currency remains static over time. In other words, inflation is not considered in the financial reports of a business, even if that business has existed for decades.

Specific Time Period Assumption

An accounting balance sheet always reports information as of a certain date. Profit and loss statements, also called income statements, encompass a date range. All financial statements have to indicate the time period for the activity reported in order for them to be meaningful to those reviewing them.

Dates are really, really important. Always check your financial statements for dates. A balance sheet will indicate the report is "as of" or "at" a certain date. Profit and loss statements will indicate they are for a specific date range.

Cost Principle

The cost principle in accounting outlines that the cost of an item doesn't change on the financial reporting. So, even if you've bought something within the year that's skyrocketed in value—let's say a building, for instance—even though its relative market value has changed, accountants will still always report the asset at the amount for which it was obtained.

Knowing this basic accounting principle definition teaches something pretty important for small business owners in general: It's important not to confuse cost with value. The value of things does change over time, and this is reflected in the gain or loss on sale of assets as well as in depreciation entries. If you need a true valuation of your business without selling off your assets, you'll need to bring in an expert in business valuations rather than relying on your financial statements.

Full Disclosure Principle

The full disclosure principle is the generally accepted accounting principle that grabs the most headlines. Under this basic accounting principle, a business is required to disclose all information that relates to the function of its financial statements in notes accompanying the statements. This principle helps make sure stockholders and investors are not misled by any aspect of the financial reports.

Going Concern Principle

Also referred to as the "non-death principle," the going concern principleassumes the business will continue to exist and function with no defined end date. Knowing this basic accounting principle will help you understand why you defer the recognition of expenses to a later accounting period. If an accountant is concerned the business might be forced to liquidate, they have to disclose this under GAAP principles.

As a new business, you need to take steps to build your business credit. Sign up for credit monitoring to stay on top of your score.

Matching Principle

For tax purposes, many small businesses choose to operate on a cash basis, meaning revenue is reported when cash is received and expenses are reported when cash is spent (or when your business's credit card is charged). But, many businesses are required to report all financial information on an accrual basis, largely due to the matching principle.

Under the matching accounting principle, sales and the expenses used to produce those sales are reported in the same accounting period. These expenses can include wages, sales commissions, certain overhead costs, etc.

Even if your tax return is on a cash basis, your accountant might prepare your financial reports on an accrual basis. Accrual basis reports reflect the matching principle and provide a better analysis of your business's performance and profitability than cash basis statements.

Revenue Recognition Principle

Under the accrual basis of accounting, revenue is reported when it's earned, regardless of when payment for the product or service is actually received. Similar to the matching principle, the basic accounting principle of revenue recognition accurately reports income, or revenue, when the sale was made, even if you bill your customer or receive payment at a later time.

Materiality Principle

The materiality principle is one of two basic accounting principles that lets the accountant use their best judgment in recording a transaction or addressing an error.

We often see the materiality principle at play when an accountant is reconciling a set of books or completing a tax return. If the account is off by a relatively small amount in relation to the overall size of the business, the discrepancy may be deemed immaterial. Immaterial discrepancies can be disregarded, but material discrepancies must be addressed. Similarly, immaterial expenses can be recognized at the time of purchase, but material expenses must be depreciated over time.

It's important here for the accountant to be empowered to use their professional opinion. Since businesses come in all sizes, an amount that might be significant—or material—for one business may be insignificant—or immaterial—for another.

Principle of Conservatism

The principle of conservatism is the other principle that lets the accountant use their best judgment in a situation. When there's more than one acceptable way to record a transaction, the principle of conservatism instructs the accountant to choose the option that's best for the business they're working with.

It's important to understand this basic accounting principle is only invoked when either way the accountant can record the transaction is acceptable. It doesn't allow the accountant to completely disregard other accounting principles.

Examples of Accounting Principles

There are some of the main accounting principles and guidelines:

- Conservatism Principle: In situations where there are two acceptable solutions for reporting an item, the accountant should 'play it safe' by choose the less favourable outcome. This concept allows accountants to anticipate future losses, rather than future gains.
- Consistency Principle: The consistency principle states that once you decide on an accounting method or principle to use in your business, you need to stick with and follow this method throughout your accounting periods.
- Cost Principle: A business should record their assets, liabilities and equity at the original cost at which they were bought or sold. The real value may change over time (e.g. depreciation of assets/inflation) but this is not reflected for reporting purposes.
- Economic Entity Principle: The transactions of a business should be kept and treated separately to that of its owners and other businesses.
- Full Disclosure Principle: Any important information that may impact the reader's understanding of a business's financial statements should be disclosed or included alongside to the statement.
- Going Concern Principle: The concept that assumes a business will continue to exist and operate in the foreseeable future, and not liquidate. This allows a business to defer some prepaid expenses (accrued) to future accounting periods, rather than recognise them all at once.
- Matching Principle: The concept that each revenue recorded should be matched and recorded with all the related expenses, at the same time. Specifically in accrual accounting, the matching principle states that for every debit there should be a credit (and vice versa).
- Materiality Principle: An item is considered 'material' if it would affect or influence the decision of a reasonable individual reading the company's financial statements. This concept states that accountants must be sure to include and report all material items in the financial statement.
- Monetary Unit Principle: Businesses should only record transactions that can be expressed in terms of a stable unit of currency.

- Reliability Principle: The reliability principle is used as a guideline in determining which financial information should be presented in the accounts of a business.
- Revenue Recognition Principle: Companies should record their revenues when it is recognised, or in the same time period of when it was accrued (rather than when it was received).
- Time Period Principle: A business should report their financial statements (income statement/balance sheet) appropriate to a specific time period.

Accounting Standard

Accounting standards (AS) are written documents and policies that provides principles for recognition, measurement, treatment, presentation and disclosures of accounting transactions in the financial statements. For example: Accounting standard on inventory will provide principles on the criteria on the basis of which inventory is recognised, what all cost will form part of inventory, how to treat those cost and how to present inventory in the financial statement and relevant disclosures.

Objective of Accounting Standards (AS)

Accounting standards have been introduced with the objective to standardise accounting practices as this will help in comparing the financial statements of different entities falling in the same industry to which such accounting standards are applicable.

These Accounting Standards (AS) are issued by an accounting body or a regulatory board or sometimes by the government directly.

Accounting Standards mainly deal with four major issues of accounting, namely:

- Recognition of financial events.
- Measurement of financial transactions.
- Presentation of financial statements in a fair manner.
- Disclosure requirement of companies to ensure stakeholders are not misinformed.

Objectives of Accounting Standards

Accounting is often considered the language of business, as it communicates to others the financial position of the company. And like every language has certain syntax and grammar rules the same is true here. These rules in the case of accounting are the Accounting Standards (AS). They are the framework of rules and regulations for accounting and reporting in a country. Let us see the main objectives of forming these standards:

1. The main aim is to improve the reliability of financial statements. Now because the financial statements have to be made following the standards the users can rely on them. They know that not conforming to these standards can have serious consequences for the companies.
2. Then there is comparability. Following these standards will allow for inter-firm and intra-firm comparisons. This allows us to check the progress of the firm and its position in the market.
3. It also looks to provide one set of accounting policies that include the necessary disclosure requirements and the valuation methods of various financial transactions.

Benefits of Accounting Standards

Accounting Standards are the ruling authority in the world of accounting. It makes sure that the information provided to potential investors is not misleading in any way. Let us take a look at the benefits of AS.

Attains Uniformity in Accounting

Accounting Standards provides rules for standard treatment and recording of transactions. They even have a standard format for financial statements. These are steps in achieving uniformity in accounting methods.

Improves Reliability of Financial Statements

There are many stakeholders of a company and they rely on the financial statements for their information. Many of these stakeholders base their decisions on the data provided by these financial statements. Then there are also potential investors who make their investment decisions based on such financial statements.

So it is essential these statements present a true and fair picture of the financial situation of the company. The Accounting Standards (AS) ensure this. They make sure the statements are reliable and trustworthy.

Prevents Frauds and Accounting Manipulations

Accounting Standards (AS) lay down the accounting principles and methodologies that all entities must follow. One outcome of this is that the management of an entity cannot manipulate with financial data. Following these standards is not optional, it is compulsory.

So these standards make it difficult for the management to misrepresent any financial information. It even makes it harder for them to commit any frauds.

Assists Auditors

Now the accounting standards lay down all the accounting policies, rules, regulations, etc in a written format. These policies have to be followed. So if an auditor checks that the policies have been correctly followed he can be assured that the financial statements are true and fair.

Comparability

This is another major objective of accounting standards. Since all entities of the country follow the same set of standards their financial accounts become comparable to some extent. The users of the financial statements can analyze and compare the financial performances of various companies before taking any decisions.

Also, two statements of the same company from different years can be compared. This will show the growth curve of the company to the users.

Determining Managerial Accountability

The accounting standards help measure the performance of the management of an entity. It can help measure the management's ability to increase profitability, maintain the solvency of the firm, and other such important financial duties of the management.

Management also must wisely choose their accounting policies. Constant changes in the accounting policies lead to confusion for the user of these financial statements. Also, the principle of consistency and comparability are lost.

Limitations of Accounting Standards

There are a few limitations of Accounting Standards as well. The regulatory bodies keep updating the standards to restrict these limitations.

Difficulty between Choosing Alternatives

There are alternatives for certain accounting treatments or valuations. Like for example, stocks can be valued by LIFO, FIFO, weighted average method, etc. So choosing between these alternatives is a tough decision for the management. The AS does not provide guidelines for the appropriate choice.

Restricted Scope

Accounting Standards cannot override the laws or the statutes. They have to be framed within the confines of the laws prevailing at the time. That can limit their scope to provide the best policies for the situation.

Accounting System

There are different types of accounting systems, and each has distinctive features. However, they all have a common purpose: to manage the financial activities of a business, such as its revenue, expenses and liabilities. In this digital age, most accountants use sophisticated systems featuring overdue payment reminders, advanced reporting capabilities, automated data backups, cloud-based services and more.

Without an accounting system in place, you'd find it difficult to get your books ready for monthly and yearly reporting, keep track of your day-to-day expenses and assess your company's financial performance. Manual calculations are obsolete and prone to human error. Computerized accounting systems, on the other hand, are accurate and make everything a lot easier. You or your team will save time and money while preventing costly mistakes.

These programs can handle all types of accounting information and generate detailed reports. You can use them to calculate the wages paid and payable to employees, record transactions, check credit turnover ratios and process data related to sales, payroll, inventory and other key aspects of your business. Some accounting systems are designed for small businesses and freelancers, while others appeal to large enterprises, government agencies or specific industries.

Types of Accounting Software

Choosing an accounting system depends on your budget, preferences and business size. The four main types of financial software systems include:

- Single-entry systems
- Double-entry systems
- Manual accounting systems
- Computerized accounting systems

These can be further broken down into several other categories, such as cloud accounting software, custom accounting software, enterprise resource planning software, commercial off-the-shelf software and more. The latest programs have marketing and sales automation capabilities, unlimited invoice scheduling, payroll modules and other cutting-edge features. Their application in accounting goes beyond tracking your day-to-day financial operations.

Single-entry systems are the most basic option. As their name suggests, they record each transaction with a single entry in the accounting journal. This method is easy to use and doesn't require training in accounting. It appeals to small companies with a low volume of activity. The downside is that it's prone to errors and doesn't track accounts receivable, accounts payable, liabilities and more.

Most types of financial software systems nowadays, including those designed for small enterprises, use double-entry bookkeeping. This means that every transaction will involve at least two accounts, which allows for more accurate reporting and timely error detection.

Manual vs. Computerized Accounting Systems

Both types of accounting systems are based on the same principles. Manual accounting, however, is time consuming and involves more paperwork. Those who use it need to prepare financial statement reports, calculate trial balances, record transactions in physical registers and so on. Since everything is done manually, there's a higher risk of human error.

Computerized systems, on the other hand, record financial transactions electronically and can streamline your operations.

Depending on your niche, you can also opt for industry-specific accounting systems, such as Sage 300 Construction and Real Estate, Abila MIP Fund Accounting or Sage Fixed Assets. Many programs are specially designed for health care facilities, manufacturing companies, nonprofits and other types of organizations.

Examples of Accounting Systems

A good accounting system should provide managerial reports, financial statements, reports prepared for outsiders and adequate information to file tax returns.

Accounting Systems for Manufacturers

Manufacturers make and assemble products, so their accounting systems should have information on inventory, labor hours, overhead expenses and sales commissions. A manufacturer can have three types of inventory: raw materials, products in production and finished products. A manufacturer also needs to know how many man-hours are used to make each product.

Payroll systems need to track at least three types of personnel: manufacturing labor by the hour, administrative staff by salary, and salespeople who are paid by commission.

Overhead expenses have to be allocated to manufacturing expenses to determine the individual costs to make each product.

Accounting Systems for Retailers

The business of a retailer consists of buying and selling products. A retailer's accounting system contains a detailed reporting of inventory. These details should include the level of inventory, the annual turnover rate, the profit of each product and reorder points. Since most retailers buy many different products, their accounting system needs extensive information on the status of accounts payable, delivery times and available discounts.

Retailers sell for cash, so they need reports on their bank accounts and credit card processing times and fees. Point-of-sale equipment should be connected directly to the accounting software for real-time reports.

Accounting Systems for Distributors

The accounting systems for distributors are similar to the ones for retailers, but distributors typically sell on credit terms to their customers, so they need beefier reports on their accounts receivable. More than likely, several people in the office need access to accounts receivable reports so they can contact customers and follow up on late payments.

Like retailers, distributors need detailed information on their inventory: the cost of each item, sales per product and the profit of each product.

Accounting Systems for Construction

Contractors have different needs from their accounting systems. They need the ability to track the costs and progress of their building projects. The accounting system for contractors should report the material costs of products going into each project, how many labor man-hours are being consumed and what is the percentage-of-completion of the project.

Contractors usually finance the costs of their projects with bank lines of credit. So, their liabilities should have information about the amounts drawn down on the lines of credit and the due dates of loans.

Accounting Systems for Nonprofits

Nonprofit organizations need to keep track of their donors to identify who is giving them money. An NPO is obligated to send end-of-year statements of their donations to the donors for use with tax filings.

The accounting systems for nonprofits should be able to produce income and expense reports for presentations to a board of directors, major donors and the government.

Nonprofit managers need reports that track contributions to individual programs versus the budgeted amounts.

Accounting systems come in a variety of forms that are modified for the distinct needs of an industry. While the main purpose of an accounting system is to track income and expenses, there are many different ways to do that. Business managers have to step back and identify their exact needs when considering accounting programs for their company. Managers need internal reports modified for decision-making purposes, financial statements for presentation to investors and creditors, and accurate data for tax returns.

Types of Accounting

There are several types of accounting that range from auditing to the preparation of tax returns. Accountants tend to specialize in one of these fields, which leads to the different career tracks noted below:

- Financial accounting: This field is concerned with the aggregation of financial information into external reports. Financial accounting requires detailed knowledge of the accounting framework used by the reader of a company's financial statements, such as Generally Accepted Accounting Principles (GAAP) or International Financial Reporting Standards (IFRS). Or, if a company is publicly-held, it requires a knowledge of the standards issued by the government entity responsible for public company reporting in a specific country (such as the Securities and Exchange Commission in the United States). There are several career tracks involved in financial accounting. There is a specialty in external reporting, which usually involves a detailed knowledge of accounting standards. There is also the controller track, which requires a combined knowledge of financial and management accounting.

- Public accounting: This field investigates the financial statements and supporting accounting systems of client companies, to provide assurance that the financial statements assembled by clients fairly present their financial results and financial position. This field requires excellent knowledge of the relevant accounting framework, as well as an inquiring personality that can delve into client systems as needed. The career track here is to progress through various audit staff positions to become an audit partner.

- Government accounting: This field uses a unique accounting framework to create and manage funds, from which cash is disbursed to pay for a number of expenditures related to the provision of services by a government entity. Government accounting requires such a different skill set that accountants tend to specialize within this area for their entire careers.

- Forensic accounting: This field involves the reconstruction of financial information when a complete set of financial records is not available. This skill set can be used to reconstruct the records of a destroyed business, to reconstruct fraudulent records, to convert cash-basis accounting records to the accrual basis, and so forth. This career tends to attract auditors. It is usually a consulting position, since few businesses require the services of a full-time forensic accountant. Those in this field are more likely to be involved in the insurance industry, legal support, or within a specialty practice of an audit firm.
- Management accounting: This field is concerned with the process of accumulating accounting information for internal operational reporting. It includes such areas as cost accounting and target costing. A career track in this area can eventually lead to the controller position, or can diverge into a number of specialty positions, such as cost accountant, billing clerk, payables clerk, and payroll clerk.
- Tax accounting: This field is concerned with the proper compliance with tax regulations, tax filings, and tax planning to reduce a company's tax burden in the future. There are multiple tax specialties, tracking toward the tax manager position.
- Internal auditing: This field is concerned with the examination of a company's systems and transactions to spot control weaknesses, fraud, waste, and mismanagement, and the reporting of these findings to management. The career track progresses from various internal auditor positions to the manager of internal audit. There are specialties available, such as the information systems auditor and the environmental auditor.

References

- Define-accounting: enotes.com, Retrieved 2 April, 2019
- Basic-accounting-terms-defined: accountingdepartment.com, Retrieved 12 July, 2019
- Elements-of-accounting, accounting-basics: accountingverse.com, Retrieved 23 May, 2019
- Accounting-process: businessdictionary.com, Retrieved 25 January, 2019
- Accounting-cycle, accounting-basics: accountingverse.com, Retrieved 8 August, 2019
- Accounting-principles: fundera.com, Retrieved 18 January, 2019
- Accounting-principles: debitoor.com, Retrieved 29June, 2019
- Accounting-standards: taxmann.com, Retrieved 9 February, 2019
- Accounting-standards-objectives-benefits-limitations, accounting-standards, principles-and-practice-of-accounting: toppr.com, Retrieved 19 May, 2019
- Various-types-accounting-systems: bizfluent.com, Retrieved 7 March, 2019
- Examples-accounting-systems: smallbusiness.chron.com, Retrieved 17 May, 2019
- What-are-the-types-of-accounting: accountingtools.com, Retrieved 20 January, 2019

2

Understanding Cost Accounting

The value of money which has been spent to produce something or to deliver a service is known as its cost. The set of procedures for the purpose of recording and reporting measurements of the cost incurred in manufacturing goods and providing services is known as cost accounting. The topics elaborated in this chapter will help in gaining a better perspective about cost accounting as well as its purpose and importance.

Cost

In a business, cost expresses the amount of money that is spent on the production or creation of a good or service. Cost does not include a mark-up for profit.

From a seller's point of view, cost is the amount of money spent to produce a product or good. If sellers sold their goods at the same price as they cost to produce, then they would break even. This means that they would not lose money on their sales, but their company would not make a profit either.

Therefore, the cost of a product from the buyer's point of view can be called the price. This is the amount charged for a product by the seller, and it includes both the cost to make the product and the mark-up cost added by the seller to produce a profit.

Cost in Accounting

In accounting, the term cost refers to the monetary value of expenditures for services, supplies, raw materials, labor, products, equipment, etc. Cost is an amount that is recorded in bookkeeping records as an expense.

Cost Accounting

Cost accounting is an accounting method that aims to capture a company's costs of production by assessing the input costs of each step of production as well as fixed costs, such as depreciation of capital equipment. Cost accounting will first measure and record these costs individually, then compare input results to output or actual results to aid company management in measuring financial performance.

Breaking down Cost Accounting

While cost accounting is often used within a company to aid in decision making, financial accounting is what the outside investor community typically sees. Financial accounting is a different representation of costs and financial performance that includes a company's assets and liabilities. Cost accounting can be most beneficial as a tool for management in budgeting and in setting up cost control programs, which can improve net margins for the company in the future.

One key difference between cost accounting and financial accounting is that while in financial accounting the cost is classified depending on the type of transaction, cost accounting classifies costs according to information needs of the management. Cost accounting, because it is used as an internal tool by management, does not have to meet any specific standard set by the Generally Accepted Accounting Principles (GAAP) and, as a result, varies in use from company to company or from department to department.

Development of Cost Accounting

Scholars have argued that cost accounting was first developed during the industrial revolution when the emerging economics of industrial supply and demand forced manufacturers to start tracking whether to decrease the price of their overstocked goods or decrease production.

During the early 19th century when David Ricardo and T. R. Malthus were developing the field of economic theory, writers like Charles Babbage were writing the first books designed to guide businesses on how to manage their internal cost accounting.

By the beginning of the 20th century, cost accounting had become a widely covered topic in the literature of business management.

Types of Cost Accounting

Standard Cost Accounting

This type of cost accounting uses ratios to compare efficient uses of labor and materials to produce goods or services under standard conditions. Assessing these differences is called a variance analysis. Traditional cost accounting essentially allocates cost based on one measure, labor or machine hours. Due to the fact that overhead cost has risen proportionate to labor cost since the genesis of standard cost accounting, allocating overhead cost as an overall cost has ended up producing occasionally misleading insights.

Some of the issues associated with cost accounting are that this type of accounting emphasizes labor efficiency despite the fact that it makes up a comparatively small amount of the costs for modern companies.

Activity-based Costing

The Charter Institute of Management Accountants defines activity-based accounting as, "an approach to the costing and monitoring of activities which involves tracing resource consumption and costing final outputs, resources assigned to activities, and activities to cost objects based on consumption estimates. The latter utilize cost drivers to attach activity costs to outputs."

Activity-based costing accumulates the overheads from each department and assigns them to specific cost objects, such as services, customers, or products. The way these costs are assigned to cost objects are first decided in an activity analysis, where appropriate output measures are cost drivers. As a result, activity-based costing tends to be much more accurate and helpful when it comes to helping managers understand the cost and profitability of their company's specific services or products. Accountants using activity-based costing will pass out a survey to employees who will then account for the amount of time they spend on different tasks. This gives management a better idea of where time and money is being spent.

Lean Accounting

Lean accounting is an extension of the philosophy of lean manufacturing and production developed by Japanese companies in the 1980s. Most accounting practices for manufacturing work off the assumption that whatever is being produced is done in a large scale. Instead of using standard costing, activity based costing, cost-plus pricing, or other management accounting systems, when using lean accounting those methods are replaced by value-based pricing and lean-focused performance measurements. For example, using a box score to facilitate decision making and create simplified and digestible financial reports.

Marginal Costing

Considered a simplified model of cost accounting, marginal costing (sometimes called cost-volume-profit analysis) is an analysis of the relationship between a product's or service's sales price, the volume of sales, the amount produced, expenses, costs, and profits. That specific relationship is called the contribution margin. The contribution margin is calculated by dividing revenue minus variable cost by revenue. This type of analysis can be used by management to gain insight into potential profits as impacted by changing costs, what types of sales prices to establish, and types of marketing campaigns.

Types of Costs

1. Fixed Costs are costs that don't vary depending on the amount of work a company is doing. These are usually things like the payment on a building or a piece of equipment that is depreciating at a fixed monthly rate.

2. Variable costs are costs tied to a company's level of production. An example could be a coffee roaster which, after receiving a large order of beans from a far-away locale, has to pay a higher rate for both shipping, packaging, and processing.
3. Operating costs are costs associated with the day-to-day operations of a business. These costs can be either fixed or variable depending on the unique situation.
4. Direct costs are costs related to producing a product. If a coffee roaster spends five hours roasting coffee, the direct costs of the finished product include the labor hours of the roaster and the cost of the coffee beans. The energy cost to heat the roaster would be indirect because it is inexact and difficult to trace.

The Principles of Cost Accounting

Cost accounting provides the management of a company with the information it needs to operate the business effectively. It differs from financial accounting in its focus on principles of costing, attributing costs to the activity that generates them and on cost reduction. Rather than producing a balance sheet based on assets and liabilities, you can use cost accounting methodology to study how your business operates and where you are spending your revenue.

Identifying All your Costs

Cost accounting generally focuses on a particular product, activity or project. It relies on the principle of collecting all the costs that fall within the area you are analyzing, no matter how they are incurred or who generates them. You use the costs collected or estimated in this way to create a budget that can guide your operations, control how much you spend and allocate resources where they will have the greatest effect. Using project cost accounting, for example, you can estimate the costs for a project, establish the project budget, control the costs as they come in and prepare a report on whether the project came in on budget.

Basic Cost Accounting Categories

Cost accounting principles designate costs either as direct costs or as overhead. Direct costs are costs you would not incur if you did not carry out the related activity. Overhead costs are fixed costs that you have to pay whether or not you complete a project, an activity or a production run. Typical direct costs are labor and material used in production, employees working on a project or designers creating a new product line. Typical overhead costs are costs for general management, human resources and company facilities. You can use cost accounting to identify separate categories such as direct labor and analyze the specific costs in each category.

Using Cost Accounting Methodology

Your cost accounting process can examine where the individual cost items in each category come from and whether the cost is justified. For example, if under direct labor you have a cost item for cutting and painting a steel sheet for use in your products, you can verify whether the cost is reasonable or whether purchasing a pre-cut, pre-painted piece of steel might be more cost effective. If your overhead costs are too high, you can look at individual items to see where the bulk of the high costs are being generated.

Eliminating Unnecessary Costs

The purpose of breaking down costs into individual items and arranging them in categories is to allow you to analyze which costs don't deliver benefits. On the overhead side, you can eliminate fixed amounts that result from expenses that don't contribute to the effective operation of the company. For example, you can sometimes cut overhead costs by eliminating unnecessary travel. On the direct-cost side, you can cut product features with high costs that don't add value for customers, streamline workflows by reducing the cost of wait times and eliminate project activities that result in functions that are not needed. Reducing direct-product costs is especially important, because the avoided per-product costs add up as production quantity increases.

Additional Cost Savings

Cost accounting can deliver additional savings when you compare the costs of specific items with industry standards or with your own historical data. If it costs you more to ship a product than other companies in your field, you have to look at what you are doing differently. If a project activity, such as installing the electrical system, costs more than it did for previous projects, you can find out why and possibly reduce the cost. Using cost accounting to keep track of your past costs and estimate future costs lets you control current costs and avoid spending more than is justified on particular items.

Concept of Cost Accounting

Cost accounting is a branch of accounting that has evolved to overcome the limitations of financial accounting. It is the process of accounting for cost, which is concerned more with the ascertainment, allocation, distribution and accounting aspects of cost. It is that branch of accounting, which deals with the classification, recording, allocation, summation and reporting of current and prospective costs. Actually, it is the formal mechanism by means of which of products and services are ascertained and controlled.

It is an internal reporting systems that aims to assist the management for planning and decision-making it primary emphasizes on cost and deals with collection, analysis, interpretation and prospective for managerial decision making on various business problems.

Cost accounting is more concerned with short-tem planning and its reporting period is much losses that financial accounting. It deals with historic data but is also futuristic in approach. Cost accounting systems cannot be installed without proper financial accounting systems. Each organization can develop a costing systems best suited to its individual needs. In financial accounting the major emphasis is in cost classification based on types of transaction e.g., salaries, repairs, insurance, stores etc. but in cost accounting, the emphasis is laid on functions, activities, processes and on internal planning and control and information needs of the organization.

From the above information definition, it can be concluded that cost accounting is accounting for cost aimed at providing cost data, statements and reports for the purposes to assists the managements in planning decision making and controlling.

Objective and Function of Cost Accounting

The main objective and function of cost accounting are mentioned below:

1. To ascertain cost: The main objective of cost accounting is to ascertain the cost of goods and services. The expenses that are incurred while producing goods or rendering services are called costs. Some examples of costs are material, labor and other direct and indirect expenses. Under cost accounting, cost are collected, classified and analyzed with the aim of finding out the total as well as per unit cost of goods, services, processes, contract etc.

2. To analyses cost and loss: Another objective of cost accounting is to analyze the cost of each activity. The analysis of cost is necessary to classify the cost into controllable or uncontrollable, relevant or irreverent, profitable or unprofitable etc. similarly, under cost accounting the effects of material, idle time, breakdown or damage of machine on the cost is also analyzed.

3. To control cost: Cost control is a technique that is used to minimize the cost of product and services without compromising on the quality. Cost accounting aims at controlling the cost by using various techniques, such as standard costing and budgetary control.

4. To help in fixation of selling price: Another important objective of cost accounting is to help in fixation of selling prices. The costs are accumulated, classified and analyzed to ascertain cost per unit. The selling price per unit is calculated by adding a certain profit on the cost per units. Under cost accounting, different techniques such as job costing, batch costing, output costing services costing etc are used for determine the selling price.

5. To aid the management: Cost accounting aims at assisting the management in planning and its importations by providing necessary costing information that also enable the evaluation of the past activities as well as future planning.

Importance and Advantages of Cost Accounting

The importance and advance of cost accounting are presented below:

1. Helps in controlling cost: Cost accounting helps in controlling cost by applying some techniques such as standard costing and budgetary control.
2. Provides necessary cost information: It provides necessary cost information to the management for planning, implements and controlling.
3. Ascertains the total per unit cost of production: It ascertains the total and per unit cost of production of goods and services that helps to fix the selling prices as well.
4. Introduces cost reduction programs: it helps to introduce and implement different cost reduction programs.
5. Discloses the profitable and non profitable activities: It discloses the profitable and non profitable activities that enable management to decide to eliminate or control unprofitable activities and expand or develop the profitable activities.
6. Provides information for the comparison of cost: It provides reliable data and information which enable the comparison of cost between periods, volume of output, determent and processes.
7. Checks the accuracy of financial accounts: It helps checking the accuracy of financial accounts. This is done by preparing cost reconciliation statement.
8. Helps invests and financial institutions: It is also advantageous to investment and financial institutions since it discloses the profitability and financial position in which they intend to invest.
9. Beneficial to workers: It is beneficial to workers as well since it emphasizes the efficient utilization of labor and scientific systems of wages payment.

Table: Differences between financial and cost accounting.

Bases of differences	Financial accounting	Cost accounting
1. Purpose	The main objective of financial accounting is to ascertain the profit earned or loss suffered by a firm during a particular period of time as well as financial position on a given data.	The main objective of cost accounting is to provide costing information to the management to facilitate planning, policy making and decision making.
2. Statues Obligation	It is statutory obligation for firm to maintain financial accounting.	It is not a statutory obligation for a firm to maintain cost accounting.
3. Users	The users of financial accounting are external to the organization like shareholders, investment, creditors, labor unions, etc.	The users of cost accounting are internal to the organization i.e. different levels of management.

4.	Pattern of analysis	It analyses the business affairs in totality.	It analyses the business affairs produces-wise, service-wise, element-wise or activities-wise.
5.	Cost control	It does not have any provision of cost control. It mealy operation and financial condition on annual basis.	Besides recording, it aims on controlling cost such as materials, labor and overhead.
6.	Period of reporting	It generally intends to reports the result of business operation and financial condition on annual basis.	It provides costing reports to the management as and when required.
7.	Orientation	It is historical in nature since it records the past transaction only.	It is historical as well as futuristic in nature since it is based on future estimations along with the past transaction.
8.	Inventory valuation	Under it, the valuation of inventory is made on the cost or market price whichever is less.	Under it, the valuation of inventory is made on cost price.

Limitations of Cost Accounting

Besides a number of advantages, cost accounting sufferers from a number of limitations. Some of them are mentioned below:

1. Lack of uniformity: Cost accounting lacks a uniform procedure. It is possible that two equally competent cost accountants may arrive at different results from the same information. Keeping this limitation in view, all cost accounting results can be as mere estimates.
2. Conceptual diversity: There are a large number of conventions and flexible factors such as classification of cost into its elements, issue materials on average or standards price, apportionment of overhead expenses, arbitrary allocation of joint costs, division of overhead into fixed and various and variable costs, division of cost into normal and abnormal and controllable and non-controllable and adoption of marginal and standard costs due to which it becomes difficult to have exact costs. In which a contacts, the reliable of cost accounting might be low.
3. Costly: There are many formalities which are to be observed by a small and medium size concerned due to which the establishment and running costs are so much that it becomes difficult for their concerned to afford us cost. Thus it can be used only by big concerned.
4. Ignorance of futuristic situation: The contribution of cost accounting for heading futures situation has not been much for example, it is has not evolved so far any tool for heading inflation situation.
5. Lack of double entry systems: Under cost accounting. A double entry system is not adopted that does not enable to checks the arithmetic's accuracy of the transaction and locate the errors.

6. Developing stage: Cost accounting is to development stage since its principle concepts and conversions are not fully developed.

Purpose of Cost Accounting

Cost accounting is utilized for a number of purposes, some of which are briefly described in the following points:

1. Accounting for costs: This may be seen as a record keeping or score keeping role. Information must be gathered and analyzed in a manner which will help in planning, control and decision making.
2. Planning and Budgeting: This involves the quantification of plans for the future operations of the enterprise; such plans may for the long or short term, for the enterprise as a whole or for the individual aspects of the enterprise.
3. The control of the operations of the enterprise: Control may be assisted by the comparison of actual cost information with that included in the plan. Any differences between planned and actual events can be investigated and corrective action implemented as appropriate.
4. Decision Making: Cost accounting information assists in the making of decisions about the future operations of the enterprise; such decisions making may be assisted by the information from cost techniques and cost-volume – profit analysis.
5. Resource allocation decisions: For example product pricing in determining whether to accept or reject jobs: This is based on cost and revenue implications of the relevant decisions.
6. Performance evaluation: Cost accounting information is used to measure and evaluate actual performance so as to make a decision of the degree of optimality or efficiency of resource utilization.

Depreciation

In accounting terms, depreciation is defined as the reduction of recorded cost of a fixed asset in a systematic manner until the value of the asset becomes zero or negligible.

An example of fixed assets are buildings, furniture, office equipment, machinery etc. A land is the only exception which cannot be depreciated as the value of land appreciates with time.

Depreciation allows a portion of the cost of a fixed asset to the revenue generated by the fixed asset. This is mandatory under the matching principle as revenues are recorded with their associated expenses in the accounting period when the asset is in use. This helps in getting a complete picture of the revenue generation transaction.

An example of Depreciation – If a delivery truck is purchased a company with a cost of Rs. 100,000 and the expected usage of the truck are 5 years, the business might depreciate the asset under depreciation expense as Rs. 20,000 every year for a period of 5 years.

Calculation of Depreciation in Small Business

There three methods commonly used to calculate depreciation. They are:

1. Straight line method.
2. Unit of production method.
3. Double-declining balance method.

Three main inputs are required to calculate depreciation:

1. Useful life – this is the time period over which the organisation considers the fixed asset to be productive. Beyond its useful life, the fixed asset is no longer cost-effective to continue the operation of the asset.
2. Salvage value – Post the useful life of the fixed asset, the company may consider selling it at a reduced amount. This is known as the salvage value of the asset.
3. The cost of the asset – this includes taxes, shipping, and preparation/setup expenses.

Unit of production method needs the number of units used during production. Let's take a look at each type of Depreciation method in detail.

Types of Depreciation Methods

There are several types of depreciation expense and different formulas for determining the book value of an asset. The most common depreciation methods include:

1. Straight-line
2. Double declining balance
3. Units of production
4. Sum of years digits

Depreciation expense is used in accounting to allocate the cost of a tangible asset over its useful life. In other words, it is the reduction of value in an asset over time due to usage, wear and tear, or obsolescence. The four main depreciation methods mentioned are explained in detail below.

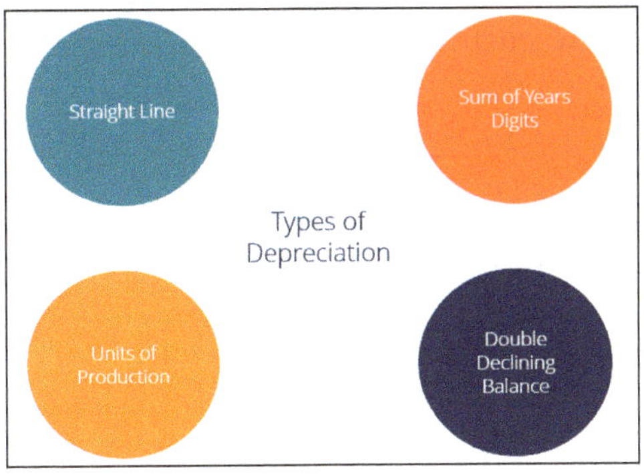

Straight-line Depreciation Method

Straight-line depreciation is a very common and simple method of calculating the expense. In straight-line depreciation, the expense amount is the same every year over the useful life of the asset.

Depreciation Formula for the Straight Line Method:

Depreciation Expense = (Cost – Salvage value) / Useful life

Example: Consider a piece of equipment that costs $25,000 with an estimated useful life of 8 years and a $0 salvage value. The depreciation expense per year for this equipment would be as follows:

Year#		**1**	**2**	**3**	**4**	**5**	**6**	**7**	**8**
Straight Line									
Opening book value		25,000	21,875	18,750	15,625	12,500	9,375	6,250	3,125
Depreciation	8	3,125	3,125	3,125	3,125	3,125	3,125	3,125	3,125
Ending Book Value	25.000	21,875	18,750	15,625	12,500	9.375	6, 250	3,125	-

Depreciation Expense = ($25,000 – $0) / 8 = $3,125 per year

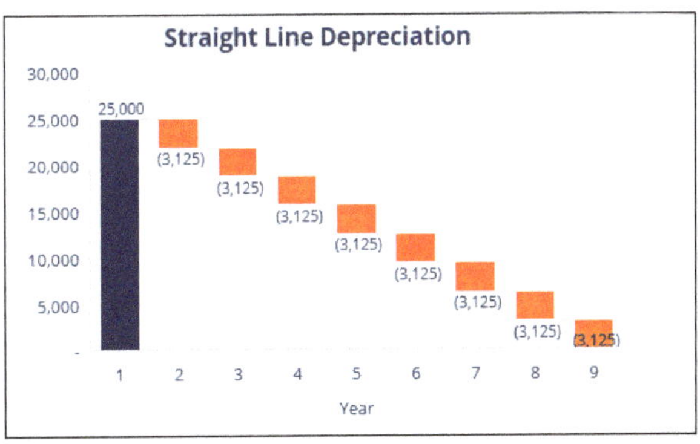

Double Declining Balance Depreciation Method

Compared to other depreciation methods, double-declining-balance depreciation results in larger expense in the earlier years as opposed to the later years of an asset's useful life. The method reflects the fact that assets are more productive in its early years than in its later years. With the double-declining-balance method, the depreciation factor is 2x that of a straight line expense method.

Depreciation formula for the double declining balance method:

Periodic Depreciation Expense = Beginning book value x Rate of depreciation

Example: Consider a piece of property, plant, and equipment (PP&E) that costs $250,000 with an estimated useful life of 8 years and a $2,500 salvage value. To calculate the double declining balance depreciation, set up a schedule:

Year#		1	2	3	4	5	6	7	8
DDB									
Opening book value		25,000	18,750	14,063	10,547	7,910	5,933	4,449	3,337
Depreciation	25%	6,250	4,688	3,516	2,637	1,978	1,483	1,112	834
Ending Book Value	25,000	18,750	14,063	10,547	7,910	5,933	4,449	3,337	2,503

The information on the schedule is explained below:

1. The beginning book value of the asset is filled in at the beginning of year 1 and the salvage value is filled in at the end of year 8.
2. The rate of depreciation (Rate) is calculated as follows:

   Expense = (100% / Useful life of asset) x 2

   Expense = (100% / 8) x 2 = 25%

   Since this is a double declining method, we multiply the rate of depreciation by 2.
3. Multiply the rate of depreciation by the beginning book value to determine the expense for that year. For example, $25,000 x 25% = $6,250 depreciation expense.
4. Subtract the expense from the beginning book value to arrive at the ending book value. For example, $25,000 – $6,250 = $18,750 ending book value.
5. The ending book value for that year is the beginning book value for the following year. For example, the year 1 ending book value of $18,750 would be the year 2 beginning book value. Repeat this until the last year of useful life.

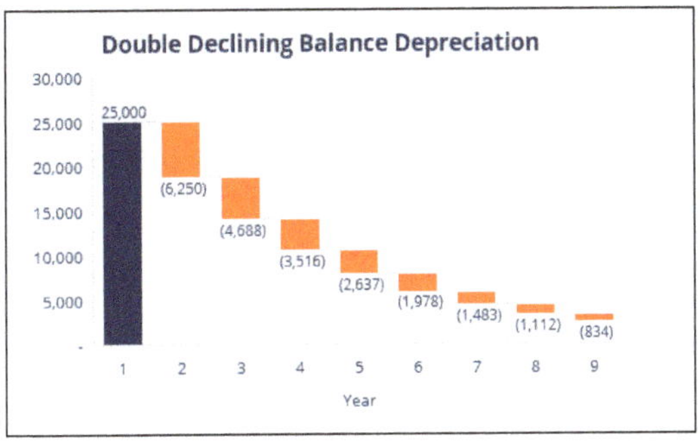

Units of Production Depreciation Method

Units-of-production depreciation method depreciates assets based on the total number of hours used or the total number of units to be produced over its useful life.

The formula for the units-of-production method:

> Depreciation Expense = (Number of units produced / Life in number of units) x (Cost – Salvage value).

Example: Consider a machine that costs $25,000 with an estimated total unit production of 100 million and a $0 salvage value. During the first quarter of activity, the machine produced 4 million units.

Year#		1	2	3	4	5	6	7	8
Units									
Production (units)		4	7	4	23	32	12	6	12
Opening book value		25,000	24,000	22,250	21,250	15,500	7,500	4,500	3,000
Depreciation		1,000	1,750	1,000	5,750	8,000	3,000	1,500	3,000
Ending Book Value	25,000	24,000	22,250	21,250	15,500	7,500	4,500	3,000	

To calculate the depreciation expense using the formula above:

> Depreciation Expense = (4 million / 100 million) x ($25,000 – $0) = $1,000

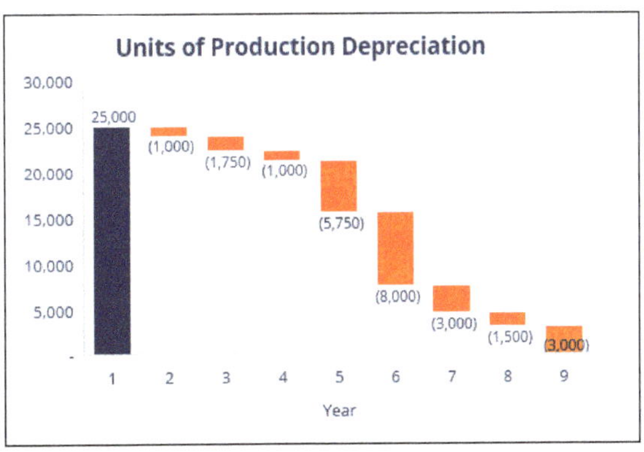

Sum-of-the- years-digits Depreciation Method

Sum-of-the-years-digits method is one of the accelerated depreciation methods. A higher expense is incurred in the early years while lower expense is incurred in the latter years of the asset.

In sum-of-the-years digits depreciation method, the remaining life of an asset is divided by the sum of the years and then multiplied by the depreciating base to determine the expense.

The depreciation formula for the sum-of-the-years-digits method:

> Depreciation Expense = (Remaining life / Sum of the years digits) x (Cost – Salvage value)

Consider the following example to more easily understand the concept of the sum-of-the-years-digits depreciation method.

Example: Consider a piece of equipment that costs $25,000 with an estimated useful life of 8 years and a $0 salvage value. To calculate the sum-of-the-years-digits depreciation method, set up a schedule:

Year#		1	2	3	4	5	6	7	8
SYD									
Remaining life		8	7	6	5	4	3	2	1
Opening book value		25000	19,444	14,583	10,417	6,944	4,167	2,083	694
Depreciation		5,556	4,861	4,167	3,472	2,778	2,083	1,389	694
Ending Book Value	25,000	19,444	14,583	10,417	6,944	4,167	2,083	694	0

The information in the schedule is explained below:

1. The depreciation base is constant throughout the years and is calculated as follows:

   Depreciation Base = Cost – Salvage value

   Depreciation Base = $25,000 – $0 = $25,000

2. The remaining life is simply the remaining life of the asset. For example, at the beginning of the year, the asset has a remaining life of 8 years. The following year, the asset has a remaining life of 7 years, etc.

3. RL / SYD is "remaining life divided by sum of the years." In this example, the asset has a useful life of 8 years. Therefore, the sum of the years would be 1 + 2 + 3 + 4 + 5 + 6 + 7 + 8 = 36 years. The remaining life in the beginning of year 1 is 8. Therefore, the RM / SYD = 8 / 36 = 0.2222.

4. The RL / SYD number is multiplied by the depreciating base to determine the expense for that year.

5. The same is done for the following years. In the beginning of year 2, RL / SYD would be 7 / 36 = 0.1944. 0.1944 x $25,000 = $4,861 expense for year 2.

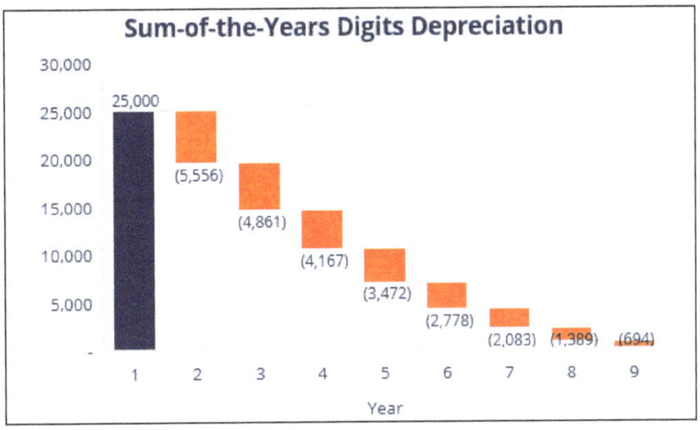

Importance of Cost Accounting

Cost accounting is a specialized branch of accounting that deals with the classification, recording, and allocation of current costs and prospective costs. In the modern commercial world, it is one of the most important techniques or process for a business. The management of an organization and its workers both greatly benefit from it. Let us see how in the importance of cost accounting.

Importance of Cost Accounting to Management

As we will see, cost accounting has many advantages. It holds importance to many different parties of business. Management, investors, employees, government and even consumers themselves benefit from cost accounting.

Let us look at some of the importance of cost accounting to the management of an organization:

1. Classification of Costs

Cost is a very generic term, it needs to be classified to be of further use. Cost accounting involves the recording and classification of such costs.

Some costs are prime cost, direct cost, factory cost, selling cost etc. Such classification allows the management to control the costs and ascertain the profitability of any such processes and activities. It also helps in calculating efficiency.

2. Cost Control

An efficient business focuses on controlling the cost of inventory, labor, and various other overhead costs. Cost accounting allows them to do so.

For example to achieve maximum efficiency in their inventory management the can adopt the EOQ technique which is a costing technique.

Similarly, by analyzing costs of labor and capacity of machinery their efficiency can be improved also. Cost accounting also classifies overheads into fixed, variable or controllable, uncontrollable to achieve cost control.

3. Price Determination

Cost accounting makes the basic distinction between fixed and variable costs. This is then used by management to fix the prices of products, according to the costs of the product.

This allows the management to find the most ideal price for the product or the service, not too high and not too low. Take for example a case where the economy suffers depression.

The businessman has to lower the prices of his products to survive these circumstances. So he can begin by trying to control his variable costs allow him to fix his prices.

4. Fixing of Standards

Organizations use standards to make estimates and budgets for the future. They use these as a basis to measure the actual efficiency of the process or department.

There is an entire branch in cost accounting known as Standard Costing dedicated to this process.

Importance of Cost Accounting to Others

1. Workers: One of the biggest uses of cost accounting is that it helps us calculate efficiency. This will help the company come up with an incentive scheme for workers who show efficiency in their work, and thus they will be awarded accordingly. It is also an incentive for workers with lower efficiency to do better.

2. Government: Costing helps the government when assessing for income tax or any other such government liabilities. It also helps set industry standards and helps with price fixing, tariff plans, cost control etc.

3. Customers: The main aims of costing are cost control and improvement in efficiency. Both of these are very beneficial to the company. And ultimately this benefit passes on to the customers of the products or services.

Importance of Cost Accounting to Business Concerns

Management of business concerns expects from Cost Accounting a detailed cost information in respect of its operations to equip their executives with relevant information required for planning, scheduling, controlling and decision making. To be more specific, management expects from cost accounting – information and reports to help them in the discharge of the following functions:

(a) Control of material cost: Cost of material usually constitute a substantial portion of the total cost of a product. Therefore, it is necessary to control it as far as possible. Such a control may be exercised by (i) Ensuring un-interrupted supply of material and spares for production. (ii) By avoiding excessive locking up of funds/capital in stocks of materials and stores. (iii) Also by the use of techniques like value analysis, standardization etc. to control material cost.

(b) Control of labour cost: It can be controlled if workers complete their work within the standard time limit. Reduction of labour turnover and idle time too help us, to control labour cost.

(c) Control of overheads: Overheads consists of indirect expenses which are incurred in the factory, office and sales department ; they are part of production and sales cost. Such expenses may be controlled by keeping a strict check over them.

(d) Measuring efficiency: For measuring efficiency, Cost Accounting department should provide information about standards and actual performance of the concerned activity.

(e) Budgeting: Now-a-days detailed estimates in terms of quantities and amounts At* drawn up before the start of each activity. This is done to ensured that a practicable course of action can be chalked out and the actual performance corresponds with the estimated or budgeted performance. The preparation of the budget is the function of Costing Department.

(f) Price determination: Cost accounts should provide information, which enables the management to fix remunerative selling prices for various items of products and services in different circumstances.

(g) Curtailment of loss during the off-season: Cost Accounting can also provide information, which may enable reduction of overhead, by utilizing idle capacity during the off-season or by lengthening the season.

(h) Expansion: Cost Accounts may provide estimates of production of various levels on the basis of which the management may be able to formulate its approach to expansion.

(i) Arriving at decisions: Most of the decisions in a business undertaking involve correct statements of the likely effect on profits. Cost Accounts are of vital help in this respect. In fact, without proper cost accounting, decision would be like taking a jump in the dark, such as when production of a product is stopped.

Role of Cost Accounting in an Organisation

Cost accountants interpret results, report them to management and provide analysis that assist decision-making in the following departments:

1. Manufacturing: Cost accountants work closely with production personnel to measure and report manufacturing costs. The efficiency of the production departments in scheduling and transforming materials into finished units is evaluated for improvements.
2. Engineering: Cost accountants and engineers translate specifications for new products into estimated costs; by comparing estimated costs with projected sales prices, they help management decide whether manufacturing a product will be profitable.
3. Systems design: Cost accountants are becoming more involved in designing computer integrated manufacturing (CIM) systems and databases corresponding to cost accounting needs. The idea is for cost accountants, engineers and system designers to develop a flexible production process responding swiftly to market needs.
4. Treasury: The treasurer uses budgets and related accounting reports developed by cost accountants to forecast cash and working capital requirements. Detailed cash reports indicate where there are excess funds to invest or where cash deficits exist and need to be financed.
5. Financial accounting: Cost accountants work closely with financial accountants who use cost information in valuing inventory for external reporting and income determination purposes.
6. Marketing: Marketing involves the cost accountant during the product innovation stage, the manufacturing planning stage and the sales process. The marketing department develops sales forecast to facilitate preparing a products manufacturing schedule. Cost estimates, competition, supply, demand, environmental influences and the state of technology determines the sales price that the product will be offered and will command in the market.
7. Personnel: Personnel department administers the wage rate and pay methods used in calculating each employees pay. This department maintains adequate labour records for legal and cost analysis purposes.

At this point, it cannot be over-emphasized that cost accounting is simply an information system designed to produce information to assist the management of an organization in planning and controlling the organisation's activities. It also assists the management to make informed decisions so as to enable the organization to operate at maximum effectiveness and efficiently.

Cost Accounting Practices in the Service Industry

Most managers associate cost accounting practices with physical products in the manufacturing industry. However, cost accounting techniques also can help service industry companies understand their costs. One difference in cost accounting practices for service companies is the terminology and construction of the cost of goods sold account. A manufacturing company's cost of goods manufactured is the sum of its material, labor and overhead costs. A merchandising company's cost of goods sold consists of the net purchase price it paid for the products. A service company's cost of services provided is primarily labor wages, overhead costs and a small amount of direct materials.

Product and Period Costs

With some tweaks, product and period costs concepts can be applied to the service industry. Standard costing differentiates product costs and period costs. Product costs are associated with product manufacturing, while period costs aren't directly associated with any product. For a service company, the product manufacturing is equivalent to delivering a specific service. For example, professional salaries and office supplies are considered product costs. Advertising, rent and insurance are considered service period costs.

Variance Factors

Variance analysis factors in product companies consist of direct materials, direct labor, variable manufacturing overhead and fixed manufacturing overhead. In the case of a service company, direct materials are the computers, office equipment and office supplies necessary to complete the service. Direct labor is the salary of the professional providing the service. For example, a lawyer's salary is considered direct labor in a law firm, while the general secretary's salary is considered an overhead cost.

Volume Variance Analysis

Although usually framed in terms of production, volume variance analysis is suitable for service companies. Volume variance equals the budgeted production volume minus the actual production volume. For a manufacturing company, this could be the number of chairs built or sofas constructed. In a service industry, this could be the number of lawsuits filed, tax returns processed or audits performed. For example, a law firm that expected to handle 50 cases and instead processed 20 would have a volume variance of 30.

Labor Variance Analysis

Because the bulk of a service industry's cost tends to be professional wages, labor variance analysis is especially beneficial. Labor variances can be analyzed by rate or efficiency. Labor hourly rate variance is the difference between the standard rate of pay and the actual rate of pay. Service companies could incur rate variances because of unanticipated overtime. For example, a law firm that budgeted to pay its paralegals $15 an hour and instead paid them $17 an hour has an unfavorable hourly variance of $2 per hour. To find the dollar value of the rate variance, multiply the hourly variance by the actual number of hours worked. In this example, if the paralegals worked 5,000 hours, the total rate variance is $10,000.

Limitations of Cost Accounting

Besides a number of advantages, cost accounting sufferers from a number of limitations. Some of them are mentioned below:

1. Lack of uniformity: Cost accounting lacks a uniform procedure. It is possible that two equally competent cost accountants may arrive at different results from the same information. Keeping this limitation in view, all cost accounting results can be as mere estimates.
2. Conceptual diversity: There are a large number of conventions and flexible factors such as classification of cost into its elements, issue materials on average or standards price, apportionment of overhead expenses, arbitrary allocation of joint costs, division of overhead into fixed and various and variable costs, division of cost into normal and abnormal and controllable and non-controllable and adoption of marginal and standard costs due to which it becomes difficult to have exact costs. In which a contacts, the reliable of cost accounting might be low.
3. Costly: There are many formalities which are to be observed by a small and medium size concerned due to which the establishment and running costs are so much that it becomes difficult for their concerned to afford us cost. Thus it can be used only by big concerned.
4. Ignorance of futuristic situation: The contribution of cost accounting for heading futures situation has not been much for example, it is has not evolved so far any tool for heading inflation situation.
5. Lack of double entry systems: Under cost accounting. A double entry system is not adopted that does not enable to checks the arithmetic's accuracy of the transaction and locate the errors.
6. Developing stage: Cost accounting is to development stage since its principle concepts and conversions are not fully developed.

References

- Cost, accounting-words, accountingsoftware: reviso.com, Retrieved 15 April, 2019
- Cost-accounting: investopedia.com, Retrieved 5 August, 2019
- Principles-cost-accounting: chron.com, Retrieved 27 July, 2019
- Cost-accounting: onlineaccountreading.blogspot.com, Retrieved 7 January, 2019
- Purpose-of-cost-accounting-information, cost-accounting: businesswritingservices.org, Retrieved 18 March, 2019
- What-is-depreciation: profitbooks.net, Retrieved 9 April, 2019
- Types-depreciation-methods: corporatefinanceinstitute.com, Retrieved 23 July, 2019
- Importance-of-cost-accounting, fundamentals-of-cost-accounting, fundamentals-of-accounting: toppr.com, Retrieved 17 February, 2019
- Importance-of-cost-accounting-to-business-concerns, cost-accounting: preservearticles.com,Retrieved 1 May, 2019
- The-role-of-a-cost-accounting-department-in-an-organization, cost-accounting: businesswritingservices.org, Retrieved 11 January, 2019
- Cost-accounting-practices-service-industry: azcentral.com, Retrieved 13 February, 2019
- Cost-accounting: onlineaccountreading.blogspot.com, Retrieved 6 June, 2019

3

Concepts and Elements of Cost Accounting

Some of the fundamental concepts and elements of cost accounting are cost principle, cost allocation, variable cost, fixed cost, short-run cost, long-run cost, labor and overheads. The chapter closely examines these key concepts of cost accounting to provide an extensive understanding of the subject.

Cost accounting is different from financial accounting:

- In traditional accounting, the profit and loss is derived by deducting expenses from income whereas in cost accounting the motive is to be cost effective by reducing costs of process, production or project.
- Financial accounting views an organization in entirety whereas cost accounting segregates the organization into various processes, projects or production units.
- Financial accounting is used to present the position of the organization to its stakeholders whereas cost accounting is used for internal review of costs.
- Financial accounting is uniform across various businesses, however, cost accounting methods vary based on the type of business.

Elements of Cost

For a standard manufacturing unit the various costs involved can be segregated into the following:

- Material
- Labour
- Other expenses

These can be further segregated into the following:

- Direct
- Indirect

Illustration: Say a toy manufacturing unit procures plastic as a raw material. The cost of plastic is direct material cost. The costs incurred in the packing and transportation of the same is the indirect material cost. Similarly, the labour cost for the production of toys is the direct labour cost whereas the salary of the production supervisor will be indirect labour cost.

Cost Principle

In accounting, the cost principle is part of the generally accepted accounting principles. Assets should always be recorded at their cost, when the asset is new and also for the life of the asset. For instance, land purchased for $30,000 is appraised at the much higher value because the housing market has risen, but the reported value of the land will remain $30,000.

Cost Allocation

Cost allocation is a process of providing relief to shared service organization's cost centers that provide a product or service. In turn, the associated expense is assigned to internal clients' cost centers that consume the products and services. For example, the CIO may provide all IT services within the company and assign the costs back to the business units that consume each offering.

The core components of a cost allocation system consist of a way to track which organizations provides a product and/or service, the organizations that consume the products and/or services, and a list of portfolio offerings (e.g. service catalog). Depending on the operating structure within a company, the cost allocation data may generate an internal invoice or feed an ERP system's chargeback module. Accessing the data via an invoice or chargeback module are the typical methods that drive personnel behavior. In return, the consumption data becomes a great source of quantitative information to make better business decisions. Today's organizations face growing pressure to control costs and enable responsible financial management of resources. In this environment, an organization is expected to provide services cost-effectively and deliver business value while operating under tight budgetary constraints. One way to contain costs is to implement a cost allocation methodology, where your business units become directly accountable for the services they consume.

An effective cost allocation methodology enables an organization to identify what services are being provided and what they cost, to allocate costs to business units, and to manage cost recovery. Under this model, both the service provider and its respective consumers become aware of their service requirements and usage and how they directly influence the costs incurred. This information, in turn, improves discipline within the business units and financial discipline across the entire organization. With the organization articulating the costs of services provided, the business units become empowered and encouraged to make informed decisions about the services and availability levels they request. They can make trade-offs between service levels and costs, and they can benchmark internal costs against outsourced providers.

Types of Costs

Every organization must define their costs, like how funding runs through the organization, who touches it, what they do and how they do it serves as a foundation for this understanding. According to the Office of Management and Budget's (OMB) Uniform Guidance, there are only three types of costs – Indirect, Indirect-Admin (Overhead) and Direct. By correctly defining and allocating costs, true cost of service can be fully captured.

1. Direct costs - Are those that can be associated specifically to a final cost objective. You know what you spend on programs. You know what expenses go directly to your mission. Most importantly, you know what expenses go directly to those benefitting from your service.

2. Indirect costs - Are things that you need to do for the sake of the organizational health & operations, but don't tie back to a specific program. For instance, the actual time (resources) that need to be dedicated when working with your Internet provider to fix the organization's connection is important, but it 's unlikely that the time spent can be tied to one particular function in a program.

3. Indirect-Admin (Overhead) costs - Are defined as those that are not Direct but are necessary for the immediate support of the program. Indirect-Admin costs or Overhead are very important to nonprofits since unlike government, they do not necessarily have separate buckets of funding. If Direct costs are the foundation, the Overhead costs are one touch away. So, when you are working on managing a program, leading those working for a program in their work or simply accounting for program expenses and revenues, you are only one touch away and are, in effect, performing direct activities. These activities can be attributed to your Direct Costs for purposes of expense reimbursement.

Variable Cost

The Variable cost is the cost proportionally related to the level of output, i.e. it increases with the increase in the production and contracts with the decrease in the total output. Simply, the cost which varies with the change in the total output is called the variable cost.

The most common form of variable costs is raw material, direct labor related to the level of output, sales commission, and the cost of all other inputs that vary with the total production. For example, if the company pays 3% sales commission for every sale made by the salesperson, then 3% is the variable cost which varies with the change in the sales volume.

The variable costs and Fixed costs together make up the total cost of the firm. Symbolically:

Total Cost = Fixed Cost + Variable Cost

The company with the higher proportion of variable costs than the fixed costs can generate higher profit margins, even at low sales. But, however, as the sales increase the profit margin generated will be less than that would have been generated with the higher fixed cost. Thus, the variable cost is essential for projecting the profits of the firm and calculating the break-even point of the business or project.

Also, the higher variable costs encourage the new entrants to enter the market, thereby increasing the competition.

Fixed Cost

The Fixed Cost is the cost that remains fixed for a certain volume of output. In other words, the cost that does not change with the change in the output or sales revenue, i.e. it remains fixed irrespective of the volume of output is called the fixed cost.

The concept of fixed cost is associated with the short run since all the costs vary over time, and no cost remains purely fixed for a longer period. It mainly includes the cost of administrative or managerial staff, depreciation of land, building, machinery and other fixed assets, maintenance cost, etc. The firm has to pay these costs irrespective of its level of production.

For example, the fixed cost would be the company's rent of the machine. Suppose a firm uses a certain machine on rent then it is required to pay rent every month, even if the machine was left idle at any point in time. Thus, the amount of rent paid every month is fixed that a firm has to incur irrespective of the usage of the machine.

The company with a relatively larger fixed cost fear fall in the profit margins, if the sales decline and conversely, if the sales increase the firm realizes higher profit margins as each additional revenue generated covers the constant cost level. Thus, the fixed cost is essential for projecting the profits and calculating the break even point of business or project.

Also, the high fixed costs discourage the new entrants from entering the market, thereby limiting the competition.

Short-run Cost

The Short-run Cost is the cost which has short-term implications in the production process, i.e. these are used over a short range of output. These are the cost incurred once and cannot be used again and again, such as payment of wages, cost of raw materials, etc.

In a short-run, at least one factor of production is fixed while the other remains variable. Therefore, in the short-run, the level of output can be increased only by increasing the variable factors such as labor, raw materials while the other factors such as capital, plant size, remains unchanged. The short-run cost includes both the fixed cost (that do not change with the change in the level of output) and variable cost (that varies with the variations in the level of output). Some factors remain fixed due to the time constraints imposed on a company.

For example, Suppose a company observes a sudden surge in the demand for its goods and in order to meet the increased demand in the short-run, it can increase its level of output only by varying the variable factors. Such as, the company can employ more labor or purchase the raw material in bulk, but however, the plant size or the machinery cannot be altered to enhance the production capacity of the firm. Thus, all the cost incurred on the variable factors such as labor and raw material constitutes the short-run cost.

From an analytical point of view, the short run costs vary with the change in the total output, but however, the size of the firm remains the same. Thus, the short-run cost is treated as a variable cost.

Long-run Cost

The Long-run Cost is the cost having the long-term implications in the production process, i.e. these are spread over the long range of output. These costs are incurred on the fixed factors, Viz. Plant, building, machinery, etc. but however, the running cost and the depreciation on plant and machinery is a variable cost and hence is included in the short-run costs.

The long-run cost is incurred when the firm decides to change its production capacity over time in order to respond to the anticipated economic profits and losses. In short-run, all the factors of production and costs are variable and hence the level of output can be changed by varying all the factors, the even capital.

In the long run, even the fixed cost becomes the variable cost as the size of the firm or scale of production increases. The entrepreneurship, land, labor, capital goods, etc. all vary to attain the desired level of profits in the long run, and the cost of each factor adds to the long-run costs.

The long-run stage is characterized by planning and implementation wherein the producer decides on the level of production and take long-run decisions that affect the overall cost of the firm. The long-run decisions include leaving or entering the market, expanding or contracting the company's operations, changing the quantity of production, etc.

Total Cost

The Total Cost is the actual cost incurred in the production of a given level of output. In other words, the total expenses (cost) incurred, both explicit and implicit, on the resources to obtain a certain level of output is called the total cost.

The total cost includes both the variable cost (that varies with the change in the total output) and the fixed cost (that remains fixed irrespective of the change in the total output). Thus, total cost includes the cost of all the input factors used for producing a certain level of output.

Often, the economists use two-factor inputs in the cost model Viz. Capital (K) and labor (L). The capital is considered to be a fixed cost, i.e. will remain fixed irrespective of the production level and per unit rental price is denoted by 'r'. Thus the total fixed cost is 'Kr'. While, the labor, denoted 'L' is considered as the variable cost, which changes in the proportion to the level of production. The wage rate is denoted by 'w' and thus, the total variable cost is 'Lw'. Symbolically,

$$TC = FC + VC = Kr + Lw$$

If it is assumed that the unit variable (labor) cost remains constant, then the total cost is linear in volume and can be calculated as:

TC = Fixed Cost + Unit Variable Cost x Amount

Implicit Cost

An implicit cost is any cost that has already occurred but not necessarily shown or reported as a separate expense. It represents an opportunity cost that arises when a company uses internal resources toward a project without any explicit compensation for the utilization of resources. This means when a company allocates its resources, it always forgoes the ability to earn money off the use of the resources elsewhere, so there's no exchange of cash. Put simply, an implicit cost comes from the use of an asset, rather than renting or buying it.

Implicit costs are also referred to as imputed, implied, or notional costs. These costs aren't easy to quantify. That's because businesses don't necessarily record implicit costs for accounting purposes as money does not change hands.

These costs represent a loss of potential income, but not of profits. A company may choose to include these costs as the cost of doing business since they represent possible sources of income.

Examples of Implicit Costs

Examples of implicit costs include the loss of interest income on funds and the depreciation of machinery for a capital project. They may also be intangible costs that are not easily accounted for, including when an owner allocates time toward the maintenance of a company, rather than using those hours elsewhere. In most cases, implicit costs are not recorded for accounting purposes.

When a company hires a new employee, there are implicit costs to train that employee. If a manager allocates eight hours of an existing employee's day to teach this new team member, the implicit costs would be the existing employee's hourly wage, multiplied by eight. This is because the hours could have been allocated toward the employee's current role.

Another example of an implicit cost involves small business owners. But some may decide to pass on taking that salary in the early stages of operations in order to increase revenues and to cut down on costs. They give the business its skill in lieu of a salary, which becomes an implicit cost.

In corporate finance decisions, implicit costs should always be considered when coming to a decision on how to allocate company resources.

Explicit Cost

An explicit cost is a cost that occurs, is easily identified, and is accounted for in the general ledger or financial statements. It represents clear, obvious cash outflow that reduces a company's bottom-line profitability. Examples of explicit costs would be items such as wage expenses, rent, or lease payments. It is easy to identify the sources of those cash outflows and the business activities to which the expenses are attributed.

Net income of a business reflects residual income remaining after all explicit costs have been paid. Explicit costs are the only costs necessary to calculate accounting profit. An explicit cost is an expense that occurs during business operations and has a clearly defined dollar amount. They are recorded in a company's general ledger and flow through to the expenses listed on a company's income statement.

Explicit and implicit costs are both utilized in the calculation of economic profit. Economic profit is the total return a company receives based on all costs incurred to attain that revenue, and it is utilized for long-term decision-making. Economic profit is used extensively to determine whether a business should enter or exit a market or industry.

Difference between Implicit and Explicit Costs

Implicit costs are technically not incurred and cannot be measured accurately for accounting purposes. There are no cash exchanges in the realization of implicit costs. But they are an important consideration because they help managers make effective decisions for the company.

These expenses are a big contrast to explicit costs, the other broad categorization of business expenses. They represent any costs involved in the payment of cash or another tangible resource by a company. Rent, salary, and other operating expenses are considered explicit costs. They are all recorded within a company's financial statements.

The main difference between the two types of costs is that implicit costs are opportunity costs, while explicit costs are expenses paid with a company's own tangible assets. This makes implicit costs synonymous with imputed costs, while explicit costs are considered out-of-pocket expenses. Implicit costs are harder to measure than explicit ones, which makes implicit costs more subjective. Implicit costs help managers calculate overall economic profit, while explicit costs are used to calculate accounting profit and economic profit.

Explicit costs, also known as accounting costs, involve tangible assets and monetary transactions and result in real business opportunities. Explicit costs are easy to identify, record, and audit because of their paper trail. Expenses relating to advertising, supplies, utilities, inventory, and purchased equipment are examples of explicit costs. Although the depreciation of an asset is not an activity that can be tangibly traced, depreciation expense is an explicit cost because it relates to the cost of the underlying asset owned by the company.

In contrast, implicit or implied costs are not clearly defined, identified, or reported as expenses. They often deal with intangibles and are described as opportunity costs, the value of the best alternative not accepted. An example of an implicit cost is wasted time, or time spent on one activity that could better be spent on another. While management will utilize explicit costs when viewing business operations, implicit costs are only calculated in decision-making or choosing between multiple alternatives.

Cost Auditing

Cost Audit is a critical review undertaken to verify the correctness of Cost Accounts and to check that cost accounting principles and planning have been efficiently followed. It is noteworthy that India is the only country which has introduced statutory cost audit to regulate about 45 vital industries of the country. Cost Audit has been defined by the Chartered Institute of Management Accountants (CIMA) of Landon as "the verification of cost accounts and a check on the adherence to the cost accounting plan."

This definition implies the following:

1. The objects of cost accounting with reference to which the cost accounting plan must have been drawn up have to be kept in mind to see whether or not the plan itself and the figures collected will lead to the achievement of the goal or objective set. For instance, if the objective is to achieve maximum efficiency, the plan and the analysis of data will be different from the case where the only objective is to fix prices.

2. It has to be examined whether the methods laid down for ascertaining costs and other relevant decisions are being implemented. Treatment and determination of abnormal losses of gains or treatment of certain expenses as direct or indirect are cases in point.

3. The correctness of the figures has to be vouched.

'Statutory Cost Audit is a system of audit introduced by the Government of India for the review examination and appraisal of the cost accounting record and added information required to be maintained by specified industries'.

The concept of cost audit has been elaborated as 'an audit of efficiency of minute details of expenditure, while the work is in progress and not a post mortem examination. Financial audit is a 'fait accomplish', cost audit is mainly a preventive measure, a guide for management policy and decision in addition, to being a barometer of performance'.

Management Auditing is the process of "auditing the quality of managers through appraising them as individual managers and appraising the quality of the total system of managing in an enterprise." Thus management audit aims at assessing how managers perform different functions of management, e.g., planning, coordinating, motivating, etc.

Advantages of Cost Audit

The chief advantage of a cost audit will be that management will be sure to get reliable data for its objectives — price fixing, decision-making, control, etc. Existence of such a system of audit will also be of great use for maintaining internal check and control and will be of great help to even financial audit. But it must be understood that the aims of financial and cost audit are different.

The former aims at prevention of frauds and errors and with presentation of Profit and Loss Account and Balance Sheet which exhibit a true and fair view of the state of affairs (of profit earned during the year and of financial position at the end of the year).

It is concerned with totality of expenditure and revenue rather than its functional analysis. Cost Audit will establish the accuracy of cost of each product, job, activity, etc., and is concerned with proper analysis of information and its estimation so that management gets the necessary information promptly. Apart from reliability of data, cost audit should afford certain incidental advantages. Rather, it should be said that cost audit will help consolidate and realize advantages expected from a system of costing. Following statement of the HR Gokhale Ex-minister of Law, Justice and Company Affairs emphasizes the social advantage of cost audit.

'The objective of this measure (cost audit) is to protect consumers from unwarranted increase in prices. Reasonableness of the prices charged can only be ensured by correct determination of costs and the margin charged by producers and their retailers. Another object underlying this step is to make the industries covered by such rules alert and efficient and also to make them know their rational cost with a view to reducing it to the extent possible. Thus by resorting to this method, the interest of consumer is safeguarded and it is definite step towards removal of social injustice'.

The advantages, briefly, are as follows:

1. A close check will be maintained on all wastages—materials in store, labour, etc.—and they will be promptly located and reported.
2. Inefficiencies in production (or efficiencies) will be located and converted into monetary terms.
3. Through fixation of individual responsibility, management by exception will be possible.
4. The system of budgetary control and standard costing will be greatly facilitated with cost audit at the hands of a qualified cost accountant.
5. Records will be up-to-date and information for various purposes will be available.
6. Cost audit may unearth a number of errors and frauds which may not be revealed otherwise. This is because a cost auditor examines expenditure minutely and compares it with standards and ascertains exact reasons for discrepancy.

Cost audit offers many advantages to management, cost accountant, shareholders, statutory auditor, consumers and the government.

These advantages are summarized below:

Advantages to Management

1. Errors in following costing principles and techniques are detected. Inconsistencies and frauds can also be detected. This keeps everyone alert and promotes efficiency.
2. Cost audit can serve to measure performance of managers and better performance can be rewarded.
3. It helps to prepare accurate cost reports and this business planning can be more accurate.

4. Inter-firm comparisons can be made with ease and this might be a very useful proposition if industrial intelligence is good.

5. Cost audit can give an idea about the comparative operational efficiency of each department of division; and may thus pin-point deficiencies and also encourage to operate in a competitive spirit.

Advantages to Management/Cost Accountant

Important advantages are:

1. His task is facilitated since errors, deficiencies, etc., are pointed out. Costing plans can be prepared to take care of these things.

2. Cost audit may help in easier reconciliation of cost and financial accounts.

3. If the cost auditor is an outsider and is an expert, he can certainly give some practical and sound advice to streamline costing systems and organisation.

4. Cost audit helps to focus attention of management on the problems faced by the cost accountant. This helps him to realize his goals and objectives with ease.

Advantages to Statutory Auditor

Important advantages are:

1. Audited cost data helps him to determine the value of stocks, remuneration of managerial personnel, etc., with ease and accuracy.

2. Data and statements of cost audit help him to prepare his audit programme and plan so that he concentrates more on those aspects which have not been adequately covered by cost audit.

Advantages to Consumers

1. The direct benefit accrues where a statutory cost audit has been done to fix a reasonable price for the consumers.

2. Since cost audit aims at ensuring efficiency in the organisation, this may also get reflected in reduced prices to the consumers.

Advantages to Labour

1. If cost audit is done thoroughly labour also stands to gain through increased profitability in the shape of bonus and other benefits.

2. Also it brings into focus the role of labour in improving efficiency in term of increased productivity.

Advantages to Shareholders

1. There is correct valuation of all kinds of inventories. This may project a true picture of the organisation before shareholders and other investors and help them to assess its performance.
2. External cost audit highlights efficiency or inefficiency, utilisation of manpower and other resources, adequacy of return, etc.

Advantages to Government and Economy

1. It helps the government to settle accounts where cost-plus contracts have been made.
2. The government can intervene to protect the interests of the consumers, labour, shareholders and investors from exploit-age or inefficient managements.
3. At the national level, cost audit promotes cost consciousness and overall efficiency. This means that every rupee invested produces the maximum quantity of goods and services.

Types of Cost Audit

The main types of Cost audit are the following:

Cost Audit as an Aid to Management

The aim is to see that all information placed before management is relevant, reliable and prompt so that management can discharge its duties well. It must also be seen that no relevant or pertinent information is suppressed.

Cost Audit on Behalf of a Customer

Often contracts are placed on "Cost Plus" basis. In other words, the customer will determine the final price to be paid on the basis of exact cost plus an agreed margin of profit. The customer, in such a case, usually gets cost accounts of the product concerned audited to establish correct cost and, therefore, price.

Cost Audit on Behalf of Government

Sometimes the Government is approached with request for financial help or protection. Before taking a decision on the request, the Government may choose to get cost accounts of the applicant audited to establish whether the need for help is genuine or is a result of mere inefficiency.

Cost Audit under Statute

The powers and duties and manner of appointment of the cost auditor are the same as that of external financial auditor and the same disqualifications will apply. The cost auditor will submit his report to the Company Law Board with a copy to the company. The right to investigate all aspects of cost accounts is presumably granted to the cost auditor.

The aim of cost audit under statute seems to be that the Government wishes to know, as an instrument of control, the costs of various goods. Government has the power to prescribe the forms in which cost audit reports are to be made out. These are designed not only to verify information, but also to convey good deal of information to Government.

Cost Audit on Behalf of the Trade Association

Sometimes trade associations seek to maintain prices at a certain level. For this purpose, the accuracy of costing information submitted by various concerns has to be checked. The trade associations may seek to have full information about production capacity and the relative efficiency of productive processes.

Elements of Cost Accounting

Cost is the value of an activity or asset. Generally, this value is determined by the cost of the resources that are expended to complete the activity or produce the asset. Although money and time are sometimes thought of as resources, they only implement or constrain the use of physical resources. The final activity or asset produced depends on what can be "afforded" given the money and time allocated to the project. Resources can be separated into four elements: equipment, materials, labor, and overhead.

Materials

The materials directly contributed to a product and those easily identifiable in the finished product are called direct materials. For example, paper in books, wood in furniture, plastic in a water tank, and leather in shoes are direct materials. Other, usually lower cost items or supporting material used in the production of in a finished product are called indirect materials. For example, the length of thread used in a garment.

Furthermore, these can be categorized into three different types of inventories that must be accounted for in different ways; raw materials, work-in-progress, and finished goods.

Materials are a very important part of business. Normally you think of material as the physical composition of the asset. However, the value of the asset may also include the cost elements of scrap material or manufacturing spares, construction form work and expendable safety items, and the cost of transporting the material to the work site. Generally, a distinction can be made between direct and indirect material cost:

- Direct material cost: All type of raw material issued, raw material purchased, transferred from one cost center to another cost center, primary packing material.
- Indirect material cost: Stores used in maintenance of machinery, building, etc., stores used by service departments, material which have very low cost.

Equipment

This represents the mechanical equipment. It is often the main cost driver for the total project, which is why it is often identified as a separate cost element. Equipment costs are part of the direct cost.

Labor

Any wages paid to workers or a group of workers which may directly co-relate to any specific activity of production, maintenance, transportation of material, or product, and directly associate in the conversion of raw material into finished goods are called direct labour. Wages paid to trainee or apprentices does not come under the category of direct labour as they have no significant value.

Often, we think of labor as the value of the work needed to complete the activity or asset; i.e. the worker's labor in painting the building or soldering an electrical contact. Labor also includes the work of the engineer who prepares the design, the foreman supervising the field work, or the technician that maintains the wave soldering equipment. Also, here a distinction can be made between direct and indirect contributions to the project:

- Direct labor: Engaged on the actual production of the product, like fabrication, installation, Equipment setting, etc.
- Indirect labor: supporting activities, engineering, supervision, etc.

Overhead

This element consists of resources needed to support the activity and/or asset. They can be broken down in the following cost categories:

- Manufacturing (factory) overhead: Includes such things as the electricity used to operate the factory equipment, depreciation on the factory equipment and building, factory supplies and factory personnel (other than direct labor). How these costs are assigned to products has an impact on the measurement of an individual product's profitability.

- Non-manufacturing (administrative) overhead: These costs are not assigned to products for purposes of reporting inventory and the cost of goods sold on a company's financial statements. However, they should always be considered as part of the total cost of providing a specific product to a specific customer. Some of the costs that would typically be included in nonmanufacturing costs include:
    - Salaries and fringe benefits of selling, general and administrative personnel. This would include the company president, vice presidents, managers, and other employees in the nonmanufacturing functions of the company.
    - Rent, property taxes, utilities for the space used by the nonmanufacturing functions of the company.
    - Insurance for areas outside of the factory.
    - Interest on business loans.
    - Marketing and advertising.
    - Depreciation and maintenance of equipment and buildings outside of manufacturing.
    - Supplies for the offices.

Overheads include:

- Production or works overhead including factory staff.
- Administration overhead including office staff.
- Sales overhead including production and maintenance of catalogues, advertising (development and purchases), exhibitions, sales staff, cost of money.
- Distribution overhead.
- Maintenance and repair including office equipment and factory machinery.
- Supplies.
- Utilities including gas, electric, water, sewer, and municipal assessments.
- Other variable expenses.
- Salaries/payroll including wages, pensions, and paycheck deductions (e.g., NI and PAYEE in the UK, FICA in the US).
- Occupancy (rent, mortgage, property taxes).
- Depreciation (durable goods including machinery and office equipment).

- Other fixed expenses.

These categories are flexible and sometimes overlapping. For example, in some companies, machine cost is segregated from overhead and reported as a separate element altogether, and payroll costs are sometimes separated from other production costs.

Types of Overheads

Overheads are costs, which are not traced directly to cost units. In other words, overhead is the total of indirect material costs, indirect labour costs, and indirect expenses. The terms 'burden', 'supplementary costs', 'on costs', and 'indirect expenses' are used interchangeably for overhead. Overheads are aggregated under some account head (e.g. supervisors' salary, office lighting, depreciation, and building up-keep) and then assigned to cost units on some equitable basis.

Overheads are usually classified in terms of functions- factory overhead, administration overhead, selling overhead, and distribution overhead. The terms factory overhead, manufacturing overhead, and production overhead are used interchangeably.

Manufacturing Overheads

Manufacturing overheads are indirect costs associated with the manufacturing process. In a product manufacturing set-up, we say manufacturing process is the sequence of operations that begin with supplying materials to workstations and end with the primary packing of the product.

In the context of producing services, the manufacturing process is the process of performing activities, concurrently or in sequence, which are directly related to creating the service. E.g., in the context of an organisation providing road transport services, manufacturing overheads are overheads associated with the operation of the vehicles. Indirect costs incurred in stores department and in departments providing support services are also included in manufacturing overhead.

Administration Overheads

Administration overheads are costs of formulating the policy, directing the organization, and controlling the operations which are not directly related to production, selling, distribution, and research or development, or any other function.

Cost of factory administration is a part of manufacturing overhead. Similarly, the cost of administration of marketing offices is a part of selling overhead.

Selling Overheads

Selling overheads are the costs associated with marketing and selling (excluding distribution) activities.

Distribution Overheads

Distribution overheads are the costs associated with the distribution of finished products. Distribution includes such activities as moving finished goods to central or local storage and moving finished goods to and from prospective customers as in case of goods on sale or return basis. In gas, electricity, and water industries, 'distribution' means pipes, mains, and services which may be regarded as equivalent to packing and transportation.

Administration Overheads

Administration overheads are expenses associated with the administration of an undertaking. Costs of formulating the policy, directing the organization, and controlling the operations of an undertaking which are not directly related to production, selling, distribution, research or development activity, or function, are administration overheads.

Thus, administration overheads do not include costs of administering manufacturing activities. Those costs are treated as manufacturing overhead. E.g., costs of operating a time office are manufacturing overheads and not administration overheads.

Examples of administration overheads are as follows- office rents and rates; expenses of office lighting, heating, and cleaning; depreciation, costs of maintenance, repair, and insurance of office building, office furniture, and office equipment; salaries to office staff; director's remuneration; office supplies and other expenses; expenses on postage, telephone, and courier services; printing and stationery; audit fees; legal expenses; and bank charges.

Administration is an independent function and is as important as the other major functions. Since no direct relationship can be established between administration overhead and products or jobs manufactured and sold, and because these costs are largely fixed in nature, they are treated as period costs and charged directly to Costing Profit and Loss Account.

Selling and Distribution Overheads

Selling overheads are costs of creating and stimulating demand and securing and executing orders. Costs of manufacturing and distributing finished products are excluded from selling overheads.

Distribution overheads are costs of moving finished products to central and local storage, moving finished products to the customers, moving finished products to and from the prospective customers as in the case of goods on sale or return basis, and making empty packages reusable.

In short, when a product is placed in a saleable condition, production function ends and distribution function begins. Overheads related to distribution function are termed as distribution overhead. Many accountants prefer to deal with selling and distribution overheads together.

Examples of selling overheads are as follows:

Salaries, commissions, travelling expenses of salesmen and technical representatives; sales office expenses; bad debts; brokerage or third-party commissions; cost of operating the marketing information system including market research; expenses on advertisement and publicity; cost of catalogues and price lists; and costs of maintenance of showrooms.

Examples of distribution overheads are the following:

Carriage and freight outwards; depreciation, cost of repair and maintenance, insurance charges, and operating costs of distribution vehicles; costs of secondary packing; warehousing expenses; expenses on insurance of finished goods; and wastage of finished goods.

Selling and distribution overheads are treated as period costs and charged directly to Costing Profit and Loss Account.

Research and Development Costs

Research is original and planned investigation undertaken with the prospect of gaining new scientific or technical knowledge and understanding. Development is the application of research findings or other knowledge into a plan or design for the production of new or substantially improved materials, devices, products, processes, systems, or services prior to the commencement of commercial production or use.

An enterprise undertakes research to increase the stock of its scientific knowledge, devices, and new applications which is expected to create competitive advantage for its business.

Research activities aim at the discovery of new knowledge which can be used in developing new products, services, processes, and techniques or in improving existing products or processes. Development starts where research ends. The results of a research cannot be put directly to commercial use. It requires feasibility study and identifying practical difficulties which may arise in its applications. Development activities include conceptual formulation, design and listing of product/process alternatives, development of prototypes, etc.

Research and development costs are likely to benefit future products and, therefore, an elaborate system of absorbing these costs to products, orders, or process is hardly justified. Where research has been undertaken at the request of a client, it should obviously be charged to the customer.

If research is specifically related to an existing product, it should be directly assigned to the product and considered in analysing the profitability of the product. Research undertaken for the general interest of the firm should be treated as period cost.

Accounting for Certain Key Items of Overheads

Bad Debt

There are two approaches for treating bad debt in cost accounts. One view is that bad debt is a financial loss only and should be excluded from cost accounts. The other view is that bad debt is similar to other expenses and should not be excluded from cost accounts.

Accordingly, bad debt is considered an item of selling overhead. Abnormally high bad debts and bad debts of exceptional nature should be excluded from cost accounts. They should be charged to the Profit and Loss Account.

Advertisement Costs

Advertisement costs should be allocated and apportioned to various functions. E.g., cost of advertisement for recruitment should be allocated to the personnel function. Costs of advertisements to create and retain demand for products and services should be allocated to selling function. Advertisement cost is an overhead but its accounting depends on its exact nature.

Advertisement cost which is likely to result in a long-term benefit should be treated as fixed asset and depreciation on the same should be treated as selling overhead, e.g., the cost of neon signs.

Market Research Costs

Market research addresses itself to specific marketing problems. This includes the study of potential markets, customer's behaviour, competitor's strategy, etc. It is like a policy cost because it does not depend on the activity level, but varies with management policy on market research.

The market research cost is treated as a selling overhead. However, if it is high in a particular period, it should be treated as a deferred charge. Only a portion of it should be included in the overhead for the current year and the balance should be carried forward to future years for inclusion in overhead costs for those years.

Royalty and Patent Fees

Royalty and patent fees may either be based on the units sold or produced, or may take the form of a periodical payment of a predetermined amount. If royalty and patent fees are fixed charges in the nature of rent, or are based on the number of units produced, they should be treated as manufacturing overheads. On the other hand, if they are based on the number of units sold, they should be treated as selling overhead.

After-sales Services

It is a common practice to offer continued free support/maintenance services during a stipulated guarantee period.

Treatment of cost of after-sales services in cost accounts depends upon the cause which has given rise to the after-sales services. If it is to rectify manufacturing defects, the cost is treated as manufacturing overhead. If design department is responsible for the defect, the cost is allocated to design department. If damage is caused in transit, the cost is treated as distribution overhead.

The following after-sales service costs are usually treated as selling overhead:

- Costs of routine services,
- Costs of after-sales services rendered only to retain customer's goodwill, even though such services are not covered under any agreement.

Appropriate accounting of costs of after-sales services requires a careful analysis of the total costs. Costs on after-sales services of an exceptional nature should be charged off to Profit and Loss Account.

E.g., if suddenly an electrical engineering company incurs an abnormally heavy expenditure in rectifying a defect in a transformer supplied to a customer, inclusion of the same in production or selling costs would distort costs of production or sales. It is, therefore, logical to charge such a heavy expenditure to Profit and Loss Account.

References

- Cost-accounting: cleartax.in, Retrieved 2 June, 2019
- Variable-cost: businessjargons.com, Retrieved 18 March, 2019
- Fixed-cost: businessjargons.com, Retrieved 9 August, 2019
- Short-run-cost: businessjargons.com, Retrieved 4 February, 2019
- Long-run-cost: businessjargons.com, Retrieved 15 July, 2019
- Total-cost: businessjargons.com, Retrieved 19 April, 2019
- Implicitcost: investopedia.com, Retrieved 29 May, 2019
- Explicitcost: investopedia.com, Retrieved 6 January, 2019
- Cost-audit-meaning-advantages-and-types, cost-audit, cost-accounting: yourarticlelibrary.com, Retrieved 16 August, 2019
- Cost-accounting-4-essential-elements: costmanagement.eu, Retrieved 28 February, 2019
- Overheads-and-its-types-with-accounting-treatment-cost-accounting, overheads, cost-accounting: accountingnotes.net, Retrieved 3 April, 2019

4

Types of Costs

Costs are broadly divided into a number of categories such as average cost, direct cost and indirect cost. Average cost is further subdivided into average fixed cost and average variable cost. All the diverse aspects of these types of cost have been carefully analyzed in this chapter.

Broadly types of costs are classified as direct and indirect, fixed and variable etc. The relationship of direct & indirect costs with fixed & variable costs is a very crucial concept to understand for doing a real interpretation of costs in any manufacturing business. At the very outset, it should be clear that all costs can be classified into direct / indirect as well as fixed /variable. In brief, we can say that any cost be categorized under one of these categories viz. direct and variable, direct and fixed, indirect and variable, indirect and fixed.

- Direct costs are those costs which are related to the product and amount of expense is easily assignable/traceable to the product. These costs are assigned to the product based on cause and effect relationship.
- Indirect costs are those costs which are related to the product but the amount of expense is not traceable in an economically feasible manner. These costs are allocated to the product based on some reasonable basis.
- Total variable cost is that cost which changes in proportion to the change in output like direct material costs. Per unit variable cost remains fixed.
- Total fixed cost is that cost which does not change in proportion to the change in output like monthly salary cost of a supervisor. Per unit fixed cost is variable.

Now let us look at those dual cost classifications:

Direct and Variable Costs

These are those costs which are related to the product, traceable and whose total cost change in proportion to the change in total output. This is very simple to understand and the best and simple example can be the direct material costs like tones of sand in preparation of tiles.

Direct and Fixed Costs

These are those costs which are related to the product, traceable but whose total cost does not change in proportion to the change in output. It is little difficult to visualize. Example for such a cost can be the salary of supervisor of tile x in the factory where tile x and y are manufactured. Here we know that the cost is incurred because we are manufacturing tile x but this cost will not increase or decrease in tandem with the change in manufacturing output of tiles as its nature is fixed for a period.

Indirect and Variable Costs

These are those costs which are not directly related to the product and therefore not traceable but whose total cost changes in proportion to the change in total output. For example, power cost at tiles factory where tile x and tile y is manufactured. Here, we know that the increase in output of any of the tiles – x or y will increase the power cost which makes it variable cost but at the same time the power cost cannot be easily allocated to tile x or tile y. It is very difficult to say how much power cost is incurred for tile x or tile y and hence it is an indirect cost.

Indirect and Fixed Costs

These are those costs which are not directly related, traceable to product but whose total cost does not change in proportion to the change in the output. It is again a simple to visualize cost. Example can be salary of the supervisor who looks after the production of both tile x and tile y. Here, we can see that the salary cost is a fixed cost which would not change with the change in output of the tiles. But at the same time, it is difficult to say how much cost of his salary is because of tile x or tile y. Therefore the cost is an indirect cost.

Average Costs

In economics, average cost or unit cost is equal to total cost (TC) divided by the number of units of a good produced (the output Q):

$$AC = \frac{TC}{Q}.$$

It is also equal to the sum of average variable costs (total variable costs divided by Q) and average fixed costs (total fixed costs divided by Q). Average costs may be dependent on the time period considered (increasing production may be expensive or impossible number in the short term, for example). Average costs affect the supply curve and are a fundamental component of supply and demand.

Short-run Average Cost

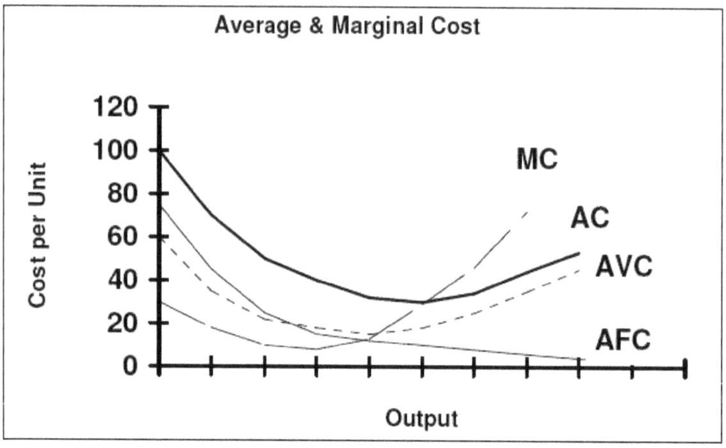

A U-shaped short-run Average Cost (AC) curve. AVC is the Average Variable Cost, AFC the Average Fixed Cost, and MC the marginal cost curve crossing the minimum points of both the Average Variable Cost and Average Cost curves.

Short-run costs are those that vary with almost no time lagging. Labor cost and the cost of raw materials are short-run costs, but physical capital is not.

An average cost curve can be plotted with cost on the vertical axis and quantity on the horizontal axis. Marginal costs are often also shown on these graphs, with marginal cost representing the cost of the last unit produced at each point; marginal costs in the short run are the slope of the variable cost curve (and hence the first derivative of variable cost).

A typical average cost curve has a U-shape, because fixed costs are all incurred before any production takes place and marginal costs are typically increasing, because of diminishing marginal productivity. In this "typical" case, for low levels of production marginal costs are below average costs, so average costs are decreasing as quantity increases. An increasing marginal cost curve intersects a U-shaped average cost curve at the latter's minimum, after which the average cost curve begins to slope upward. For further increases in production beyond this minimum, marginal cost is above average costs, so average costs are increasing as quantity increases. For example: for a factory designed to produce a specific quantity of widgets per period—below a certain production level, average cost is higher due to under-used equipment, and above that level, production bottlenecks increase average cost.

Long-run Average Cost

Long-run average cost is the unit cost of producing a certain output when all inputs, even physical capital, are variable. The behavioral assumption is that the firm will choose that combination of inputs that produce the desired quantity at the lowest possible cost.

A long-run average cost curve is typically downward sloping at relatively low levels of output and upward or downward sloping at relatively high levels of output. Most commonly, the long-run average cost curve is U-shaped, by definition reflecting economies of scale where negatively sloped and diseconomies of scale where positively sloped.

If the firm is a perfect competitor in all input markets, and thus the per-unit prices of all its inputs are unaffected by how much of the inputs the firm purchases, then it can be shown that at a particular level of output, the firm has economies of scale (i.e., is operating in a downward sloping region of the long-run average cost curve) if and only if it has increasing returns to scale, the latter being exclusively a feature of the production function. Likewise, it has diseconomies of scale (is operating in an upward sloping region of the long-run average cost curve) if and only if it has decreasing returns to scale, and has neither economies nor diseconomies of scale if it has constant returns to scale. With perfect competition in the output market the long-run market equilibrium will involve all firms operating at the minimum point of their long-run average cost curves (i.e., at the borderline between economies and diseconomies of scale).

If, however, the firm is not a perfect competitor in the input markets, then the above conclusions are modified. For example, if there are increasing returns to scale in some range of output levels, but the firm is so big in one or more input markets that increasing its purchases of an input drives up the input's per-unit cost, then the firm could have diseconomies of scale in that range of output levels. Conversely, if the firm is able to get bulk discounts of an input, then it could have economies of scale in some range of output levels even if it has decreasing returns in production in that output range.

In some industries, long-run average cost is always declining (economies of scale exist indefinitely). This means that the largest firm tends to have a cost advantage, and the industry tends naturally to become a monopoly, and hence is called a natural monopoly. Natural monopolies tend to exist in industries with high capital costs in relation to variable costs, such as water supply and electricity supply.

Relationship to Marginal Cost

When average cost is declining as output increases, marginal cost is less than average cost. When average cost is rising, marginal cost is greater than average cost. When average cost is neither rising nor falling (at a minimum or maximum), marginal cost equals average cost.

Other special cases for average cost and marginal cost appear frequently:

- Constant marginal cost/high fixed costs: Each additional unit of production is produced at constant additional expense per unit. The average cost curve slopes down continuously, approaching marginal cost. An example is hydroelectric generation, which has no fuel expense, limited maintenance expenses and a high up-front fixed cost (ignoring irregular maintenance costs or useful lifespan). Industries with fixed marginal costs, such as electrical transmission networks, may meet the conditions for a natural monopoly, because once capacity is built, the marginal cost to the incumbent of serving an additional customer is always lower than the average cost for a potential competitor. The high fixed capital costs are a barrier to entry.

- Two popular pricing mechanisms are average cost pricing (or rate of return regulation) and marginal cost pricing. A monopoly produces where its average cost curve meets the market demand curve under average cost pricing, referred to as the average cost pricing equilibrium.
- Minimum efficient scale: Marginal or average costs may be nonlinear, or have discontinuities. Average cost curves may therefore only be shown over a limited scale of production for a given technology. For example, a nuclear plant would be extremely inefficient (high average cost) for production in small quantities. Similarly, its maximum output for any given time period may essentially be fixed, and production above that level may be technically impossible, dangerous or extremely costly. The long run elasticity of supply are higher, as new plants could be built and brought on-line.
- Zero fixed costs (long-run analysis) and constant marginal cost: Since there are no economies of scale, average cost is equal to the constant marginal cost.

Relationship between AC, AFC, AVC and MC

- The Average Fixed Cost curve (AFC) starts from a height and goes on declining continuously as production increases.
- The Average Variable Cost curve, Average Cost curve and the Marginal Cost curve start from a height, reach the minimum points, then rise sharply and continuously.
- The Average Fixed Cost curve approaches zero asymptotically. The Average Variable Cost curve is never parallel to or as high as the Average Cost curve due to the existence of positive Average Fixed Costs at all levels of production; but the Average Variable Cost curve asymptotically approaches the Average Cost curve from below.
- The Marginal Cost curve always passes through the minimum points of the Average Variable Cost and Average Cost curves, though the Average Variable Cost curve attains the minimum point prior to that of the Average Cost curve.

Average Fixed Cost

In economics, average fixed cost (AFC) is the fixed costs of production (FC) divided by the quantity (Q) of output produced. Fixed costs are those costs that must be incurred in fixed quantity regardless of the level of output produced.

$$AFC = \frac{FC}{Q}.$$

Average fixed cost is fixed cost per unit of output. As the total number of units of the good produced increases, the average fixed cost decreases because the same amount of fixed costs is being spread over a larger number of units of output.

Average variable cost plus average fixed cost equals average total cost:

$$ATC = AVC + AFC$$

Example: Assume a firm produces clothing. When the quantity of the output varies from 5 shirts to 10 shirts, fixed cost would be 30 dollars. In this case, average fixed cost of producing 5 shirts would be 30 dollars divided by 5 shirts, which is 6 dollars. In other words, when 5 shirts are produced, 30 dollars of fixed cost would spread and result in 6 dollars per shirt. Similarly, average fixed cost of producing 10 shirts would be 3 dollars derived from 30 dollars divided by 10 shirts.

Fixed cost and average fixed cost at a company

Quantity (unit)	FC ($)	AFC ($)
5	30	6.00
6	30	5.00
7	30	4.29
8	30	3.75
9	30	3.33
10	30	3.00

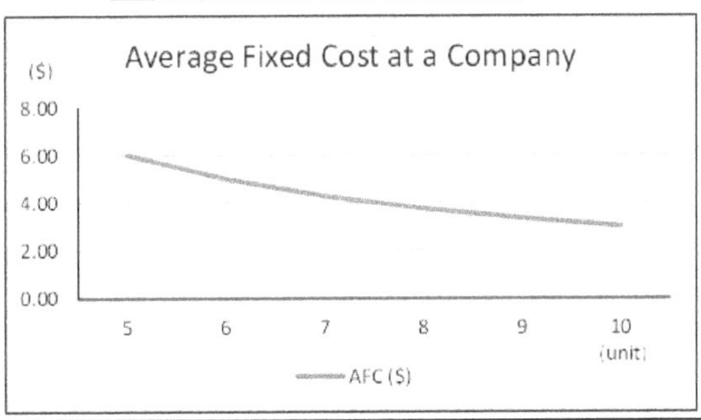

A table and graph of average fixed cost

Example: In Example1, there was no information about average total cost and average variable cost. If the firm knows average total cost and average variable cost, it is possible to find the same result as Example 1. Because average total cost is average variable cost plus average fixed cost, average fixed cost is average total cost minus average variable cost. If producing 5 shirts generates average total cost of 11 dollars and average variable cost of 5 dollars, fixed cost would be 6 dollars. Similarly, the firm produces 10 shirts and average total cost and average variable cost is 10 dollars and 7 dollars respectively. In this case, average fixed cost would be 3 dollars.

Average Variable Cost

In economics, average variable cost (AVC) is a firm's variable costs (labour, electricity, etc.) divided by the quantity of output produced. Variable costs are those costs which vary with the output level:

$$AVC = \frac{VC}{Q},$$

where, VC = variable cost, AVC = average variable cost, and Q = quantity of output produced.

Average variable cost plus average fixed cost equals average total cost:

$$AVC + AFC = ATC.$$

A firm would choose to shut down if average revenue is below average variable cost at the profit-maximizing positive level of output. Producing anything would not generate revenue significant enough to offset the associated variable costs; producing some output would add losses (additional costs in excess of revenues) to the costs inevitably being incurred (the fixed costs). By not producing, the firm loses only the fixed costs.

Direct Costs

A direct cost is a price that can be completely attributed to the production of specific goods or services. Some costs, such as depreciation or administrative expenses, are more difficult to assign to a specific product, and therefore, are considered to be indirect costs. A direct cost can be considered a variable cost if it is inconsistent and often fluctuates in amount.

Breaking down Direct Cost

Direct costs are one of two general branches of product costs in accounting for manufactured goods. The other branch, which contains all non-traceable expenses, are indirect costs. Examples of direct costs include manufacturing supplies and commissions. Rent expense may only be a direct cost if only one cost object relates to the facility being rented.

Because direct costs can be specifically traced to a product, direct costs do not need to be allocated to a product, department or other cost object. Direct costs may be related to labor, materials, fuel or power consumption. Direct costs usually benefit only one cost object. Items that are not direct costs are pooled and allocated based on cost drivers.

Fixed vs. Variable

Direct costs do not need to be fixed in nature, as their unit cost may change over time or depending on the quantity being utilized. An example is the salary of a supervisor that worked on a single project. This cost may be directly attributed to the project and relates to a fixed dollar amount. Materials that were used to build the product, such as wood or gasoline, may be directly traced but do not contain a fixed dollar amount. This is because the quantity of the supervisor's salary is known, while the unit production levels are variable based upon sales.

Direct Labor Cost

Direct labor cost is a part of wage-bill or payroll that can be specifically and consistently assigned to or associated with the manufacture of a product, a particular work order, or provision of a service. Also, we can say it is the cost of the work done by those workers who actually make the product on the production line.

1. Determination of the direct labor cost:

- Planning the work to be performed.
- Describing the job content of the work, by indicating the skill, knowledge, etc.
- Matching the jobs with the employees.

2. Usage: The direct labor cost is part of the manufacturing cost.

3. Calculation of Direct Labor Cost: In the direct labor cost we need to have the job time and wage we will pay it to the worker to calculate the direct labor cost as in this formulation:

$$\text{Direct labor cost} = \text{job time} \times \text{wage}$$

Wage

The wage is the payment rendered to the worker per hour as a compensation for the work done.

Direct Materials Cost

Direct materials cost the cost of direct materials which can be easily identified with the unit of production. For example, the cost of glass is a direct materials cost in light bulb manufacturing.

The manufacture of products or goods required material as the prime element. In general, these materials are divided into two categories. These categories are direct materials and indirect materials.

Direct materials are also called productive materials, raw materials, raw stock, stores and only materials without any descriptive title.

Direct Materials Cost Estimation

Steps to estimate the direct material costs:

1. Find the total amount to be produced. This is usually noted as the order size.
2. Calculate the total amount of raw materials required to produce the order size.
3. Multiply that amount by the cost associated with the raw materials.
4. If there is a waste or scrap, its cost should be added to the costs in step 3.
5. If the waste or scrap can be sold at salvage value, this value should be subtracted from the costs in step 4.

Indirect Costs

In simpler terms, indirect costs are those costs not readily identified with a specific project or organizational activity but incurred for the joint benefit of both projects and other activities. Indirect costs are usually grouped into common pools and charged to benefiting objectives through an allocation process/indirect cost rate.

An indirect cost rate is simply a device for determining fairly and expeditiously the proportion of general (non-direct) expenses that each project will bear. It is the ratio between the total indirect costs of an applicant and some equitable direct cost base.

Indirect Costs Ratio

$$\frac{\text{Indirect Cost Pool}}{\text{Direct Cost Base}} = \text{Indirect Cost Rate}$$

Indirect costs include costs which are frequently referred to as overhead expenses (for example, rent and utilities) and general and administrative expenses (for example, officers' salaries, accounting department costs and personnel department costs).

Commercial (for-profit) organizations usually treat "fringe benefits" as indirect costs. These fringe benefits are applied to direct salaries charged to projects either through a fringe benefit rate or as part of an overhead/indirect cost rate. Therefore, fringe benefits treated as indirect costs should not be included as a direct cost in the "Personnel" category of the budget form of the grant application or on a contract proposal.

The indirect cost base or bases (that is, the denominator(s) of the fraction producing a rate) should be selected so as to permit an equitable distribution of indirect costs to the benefiting cost objectives.

Generally, indirect cost rate structures for commercial organizations follow a single, two-rate (for example, fringe and overhead rates), or three-rate (for example, fringe, overhead, and General and Administrative expense rates) system. A single rate structure is illustrated below.

Indirect Cost Pool		
Vacation, Holiday and Sick Leave	$30,000	
Health Insurance	$18,000	
FICA Taxes	$26,000	
Pension Costs	$30,000	
Indirect Salaries	$40,000	
Facility Rental Costs	$15,000	
Equipment Depreciation	$5,000	
Utilities	$3,500	
Indirect Supplies	$2,500	
Legal Fees	$2,000	
Accounting Fees	$2,000	
Total Indirect Costs	$174,000	(c)
Direct Cost Base		
Direct Labor Costs (Salaries and Wages excluding vacation, holiday and sick leave)*	$300,000	(a)
Other Direct Costs*	$100,000	
Total Direct Costs	$400,000	(b)
Indirect Rates		
Indirect Rate Based on Direct Labor	58.0%	(c/a)
Indirect Rate Based on Total Direct Costs	43.5%	(c/b)

* Includes costs associated with independent (self-sponsored) research and development (IR&D) activities.

Indirect costs are costs that are not directly accountable to a cost object (such as a particular project, facility, function or product). Indirect costs may be either fixed or variable.

Indirect costs include administration, personnel and security costs. These are those costs which are not directly related to production. Some indirect costs may be overhead. But some overhead costs can be directly attributed to a project and are direct costs.

There are two types of indirect costs. One are the fixed indirect costs which contains activities or costs that are fixed for a particular project or company like transportation of labor to the working site, building temporary roads, etc. The other are recurring indirect costs which contains activities that repeat for a particular company like maintenance of records or payment of salaries.

Indirect vs. Direct Costs

Most cost estimates are broken down into direct costs and indirect costs.

Direct costs are directly attributable to the object and it is financially feasible to do so. In construction, the costs of materials, labor, equipment, etc., and all directly involved efforts or expenses for the cost object are direct costs. In manufacturing or other non-construction industries the portion of operating costs that is directly assignable to a specific product or process is a direct cost. Direct costs are those for activities or services that benefit specific projects, for example salaries for project staff and materials required for a particular project. Because these activities are easily traced to projects, their costs are usually charged to projects on an item-by-item basis.

Indirect costs are, but not necessarily, not directly attributable to a cost object. It should be financially infeasible to do so. Indirect costs are typically allocated to a cost object on some basis. In construction, all costs which are required for completion of the installation, but are not directly attributable to the cost object are indirect, such as overhead. In manufacturing, costs not directly assignable to the end product or process are indirect. These may be costs for management, insurance, taxes, or maintenance, for example. Indirect costs are those for activities or services that benefit more than one project. Their precise benefits to a specific project are often difficult or impossible to trace. For example, it may be difficult to determine precisely how the activities of the director of an organization benefit a specific project. Indirect costs do not vary substantially within certain production volumes or other indicators of activity, and so they may sometimes be considered to be fixed costs.

It is possible to justify the handling of almost any kind of cost as either direct or indirect. Labor costs, for example, can be indirect, as in the case of maintenance personnel and executive officers; or they can be direct, as in the case of project staff members. Similarly, materials such as miscellaneous supplies purchased in bulk—pencils, pens, paper—are typically handled as indirect costs, while materials required for specific projects are charged as direct costs.

Examples: The same cost can be labeled as indirect in one industry and direct in another. For example, fuel cost in a telecom is usually allocated as an indirect cost, while for an airliner it is a direct cost.

Costs usually charged directly:

- Salary/wages
- Consultants
- Materials
- Tools
- Transport
- Labor
- Direct materials
- PPC
- Any kind of subcontract which is attributable to direct works but the specific company does not possess the required skill

Costs either charged directly or allocated indirectly:

- Directors Salary (this is usually an indirect cost)
- Electricity (mostly if it needs allocation it is always indirect)

If electricity is not used as primary source for production then electricity cost will be treated as utility and is always indirect. For example, if electricity is required to run the boiler which in turn generates steam, then electricity needs to be allocated directly.

Costs usually allocated indirectly:

- Indirect costs related to transport
- Administration cost
- Selling & distribution cost
- Office cost
- Security cost

Indirect Cost Rate Calculation

In order to determine Indirect cost, you need to use cost allocation. Cost allocation is the process of distributing your indirect costs among specific departments or projects.

You can use the indirect rate calculation to price your products. You want your offerings to generate enough money to cover your expenses. By considering your indirect and direct expenses, you can determine a reasonable cost for your products or services so you don't underprice.

Another reason to use the indirect cost rate formula is so you can decide whether your expenses are too much. If your indirect costs are too high, you can find ways to reduce your expenses.

You can allocate indirect costs by taking your total indirect expenses and dividing them by some sort of allocation measure, like direct labor expenses, direct machine costs, or direct material costs.

Here is the indirect cost formula, or overhead rate:

Indirect Rate = Indirect Costs / Allocation Measure

The formula gives you a ratio. Let's say that you want to find your overhead rate using your direct labor expenses.

Your total indirect costs are $10,000 and your direct labor expenses are $5,000. Your formula would look like:

Indirect Rate = $10,000 / $5,000

In this example, your indirect rate is 2:1, meaning you spend $2 of overhead per $1 of direct labor expenses. The lower your indirect rate, the better.

How to Reduce Indirect Expenses

Knowing how to reduce expenses in business is essential if you need to increase your profits. You can reduce your indirect expenses using the following strategies.

Compare vendors to make sure you are getting the best deal. Expenses like office supplies can vary from provider to provider, so see if there are others who are less expensive.

If you want to reduce indirect expenses like utilities, cut your bills down by conserving energy. You can power down equipment when you aren't using it, purchase energy-conserving equipment, or switch utility providers.

You can reduce other indirect costs, like advertising, by engaging customers through social media or using other inexpensive marketing ideas.

There are many ways you can reduce your indirect expenses. Consider how valuable the expense is to operating your business and come up with ways to slash the price.

Direct Costs vs. Indirect Costs

For budgeting and accounting purposes, it's crucial not only to document your business expenses but to classify them properly. The distinction between "direct" and "indirect" costs may appear intuitive and self-explanatory. While it's true neither word takes on a dramatically different meaning when categorizing the various costs of doing business, there's a bit more nuance in practice.

Direct costs are traceable to the production of a specific good or service. The operative word is "specific." Indirect costs may be necessary to production, but they are not traceable to the act of production. Indirect costs are those necessary to keep your business in operation. Think of them as the prerequisites for the production of any specific good or service.

It's important to have a solid understanding of the distinction between direct and indirect costs when pricing your products. When you know the true costs of production, you can price both competitively and accurately. You'll also demonstrate, more clearly, the efficiency of your business practices to potential investors. The distinction is equally important when filing your tax returns. You'll save time, and more than likely, money: Certain costs, both direct and indirect, are tax-deductible.

Direct Costs

Direct costs are expenses that a company can easily connect to a specific "cost object," which may be a product, department or project. This includes items such as software, equipment and raw materials. It can also include labor, assuming the labor is specific to the product, department or project.

For example, if an employee is hired to work on a project, either exclusively or for an assigned number of hours, their labor on that project is a direct cost. If your company develops software and needs specific pregenerated assets, such as purchased frameworks or development applications, those are direct costs.

Labor and direct materials, which are used in creating a specific product, constitute the majority of direct costs. For example, to create its product, an appliance maker requires steel, electronic components and other raw materials. Two popular ways of tracking these costs, determining whether and when your company actually uses materials in production, include last in, first out (LIFO) or first in, first out (FIFO). This can be helpful when the costs of materials fluctuate in the course of production.

The majority of direct costs are variable. When direct costs vary, it's because they increase as additional units of a product or service are created. For example, smartphone hardware is a direct, variable cost because its production depends on the number of units ordered. A notable exception is direct labor costs, which are usually fixed, and remain constant throughout the year. Typically, an employee's wages do not increase or decrease in direct relation to the quantity of a product.

Indirect Costs

Indirect costs go beyond the expenses associated with creating a particular product to include the price of maintaining the entire company. These overhead costs are the ones left over after direct costs have been computed, and are sometimes referred to as the "real" costs of doing business.

The materials and supplies needed for the company's day-to-day operations are examples of indirect costs. These include items such as cleaning supplies, utilities, office equipment rental, desktop computers and cell phones. While these items contribute to the company as a whole, they are not assigned to the creation of any one service.

Indirect labor costs make the production of cost objects possible but aren't assigned to a specific product. For example, clerical assistants who maintain the office support the company as a whole instead of just one product line. Thus, their labor can be counted as an indirect cost.

Other common indirect costs include advertising and marketing, communication, "fringe benefits," such as an employee gym, and accounting and payroll services.

Much like direct costs, indirect costs can be both fixed and variable. Fixed indirect costs include things like the rent paid for the building in which a company operates. Variable costs include the ever-changing costs of electricity and gas.

Classifying Expenses

Organizing business expenses as either direct costs or indirect costs is a matter that goes beyond simple product pricing – it affects your tax payments, too. Overhead expenses, such as the utilities that power equipment and the inventory needed to manage the office, are tax-deductible. In some cases, even the costs of goods sold qualify for deductions; they reflect expenses incurred from selling products. It can be tempting to misclassify direct costs as indirect, but this can get you in a lot of trouble if you're audited by the IRS.

In cases of government grants or other forms of external funding, identifying direct and indirect costs becomes doubly important. Such programs are often strict about what constitutes a direct or an indirect cost and will allocate different amounts of funding to each classification.

Often funding is for a specific project and will largely support direct costs. Certain funders will allow companies the opportunity to justify the necessity of indirect costs for specific projects, but they will expect honesty and rigor, and the decision to grant funding as requested is still at their ultimate discretion.

For many companies, costs such as consultants, travel, communication, postage and printing, and computers may fall into a gray area. It may be difficult for a company to quantify their use of these resources for a designated purpose. In those instances, to determine whether it is a direct or indirect cost, each company should carefully consider if they need these costs for day-to-day operations or for a specific project, department or product.

Once expenses are classified, many companies calculate the indirect cost rate, sometimes called the overhead rate, to determine how to allocate administrative costs between programs or departments.

For each program or department, the indirect cost rate is the proportion of applicable direct costs to the company's total indirect costs. The company can then determine what percentage of indirect costs each program or department should bear.

In an effort to maintain efficiency and transparency, some companies set a target value for the indirect cost rate. If a department's indirect costs exceed 20 percent of the direct costs, the company may investigate the department or product to determine if the proportion should be lower. When a company accepts government funds, the funding agency may also mandate a maximum indirect cost rate for the department or project.

References

- Types-of-costs, costing-terms: efinancemanagement.com, Retrieved 23 March, 2019
- Directcost: investopedia.com, Retrieved 29 July, 2019
- Dorman, Peter (2014). "Production Costs and the Theory of Supply". Microeconomics. Springer Texts in Business and Economics. Springer, Berlin, Heidelberg. pp. 249–274. doi:10.1007/978-3-642-37434-0_12. ISBN 9783642374333
- Indirect-cost-definition-and-example, indirect-cost-submission, indirect-cost-branch: oamp.od.nih.gov, Retrieved 9 January, 2019
- What-is-an-indirect-cost, accounting: patriotsoftware.com, Retrieved 19 August, 2019
- Direct-costs-indirect-costs: businessnewsdaily.com, Retrieved 7 May, 2019

5

Types and Methods of Cost Accounting

There are a number of different methods and types of cost accounting. Some of them are activity-based costing, standard cost accounting, marginal costing, lean accounting and target costing. These topics have been carefully elaborated in this chapter to provide a holistic understanding of the subject.

Types of Costing

Before going into the types of cost accounting, let's learn about the different types of costs. In cost accounting, costs are classified into the following four types:

1. Fixed Costs: These are costs that do not vary according to the amount of work done. They include expenses like the payment made for the purchase of a building.
2. Variable Costs: These are costs that vary according to the amount of work done. They include costs like packaging, shipping and processing costs.
3. Operating Costs: These are costs associated with the day-to-day running of the business. They can be either fixed or variable.
4. Direct Costs: These are the costs directly related to producing, acquiring and selling the company's products. They include things like labour costs and electricity costs.

Types of Cost Accounting

There are mainly four types of cost accounting: standard cost accounting, activity based accounting, lean accounting and marginal costing.

Standard Cost Accounting

This type of cost accounting uses different types of ratios to compare how efficiently labour and materials are being used (or can be used) to produce goods and services in standard conditions. One of the issues associated with standard cost accounting is that it emphasizes labour efficiency even though labour costs make up small percentage of costs in modern companies.

Activity-based Cost Accounting

This type of cost accounting is defined as "An approach to the costing and monitoring of activities which involves tracing resource consumption and costing final outputs, resources assigned to activities, and activities to cost objects based on consumption estimates." It involves accumulating the overheads from each department and assigning them to specific cost objects, such as products, services and customers. Activity based costing is considered to be more accurate and, as such, more useful to managers in understanding the cost and profitability of their company's products and services.

Lean Accounting

An extension of the philosophy of lean manufacturing and production developed by Japanese companies, lean accounting emphasizes on value-based pricing and lean-focused performance measurements.

Marginal Costing

Also called cost-volume-profit analysis, this type of cost accounting involves analysing the relationship between the company's products, sales volume, production amount, profits, costs and expenses. This relationship is known as the contribution margin, which is calculated by subtracting the variable cost from revenue, dividing the remainder by revenue. It gives the management a useful insight into potential profits, the most profitable sales price and type of marketing needed.

In cost accounting, money is viewed as the economic factor of production. In contrast, money is viewed as the measure of economic performance in financial accounting. Because cost accounting is used as an internal management tool, it does not have to adhere to any specific standards and varies from one company to another.

Different Methods of Costing

Here's a breakdown of each different method of costing:

- Unit costing: This method is also known as "single output costing." This method of costing is used for products that can be expressed in identical quantitative units. Unit costing is suitable for products that are manufactured by continuous manufacturing activity: for example, brick making, mining, cement manufacturing, dairy operations, or flour mills. Costs are ascertained for convenient units of output.
- Job costing: Under this method, costs are ascertained for each work order separately as each job has its own specifications and scope. Job costing is used,

for example, in painting, car repair, decoration, and building repair.

- Contract costing: Contract costing is performed for big jobs involving heavy expenditure, long periods of time, and often different work sites. Each contract is treated as a separate unit for costing. This is also known as terminal costing. Projects requiring contract costing include construction of bridges, roads, and buildings.
- Batch costing: This method of costing is used where units produced in a batch are uniform in nature and design. For the purpose of costing, each batch is treated as an individual job or separate unit. Industries like bakeries and pharmaceuticals usually use the batch costing method.
- Operating costing or service costing: Operating or service costing is used to ascertain the cost of particular service-oriented units, such as nursing homes, busses, or railways. Each particular service is treated as a separate unit in operating costing. In the case of a nursing home, a unit is treated as the cost of a bed per day, while, for busses, operating cost for a kilometer is treated as a unit.
- Process costing: This kind of costing is used for products that go through different processes. For example, the manufacturing of clothes involves several processes. The first process is spinning. The output of that spinning process, yarn, is a finished product which can either be sold on the market to weavers, or used as a raw material for a weaving process in the same manufacturing unit. To find out the cost of the yarn, one needs to determine the cost of the spinning process. In the second step, the output of the weaving process, cloth, can also can be sold as a finished product in the market. In this case, the cost of cloth needs to be evaluated. The third process is converting the cloth to a finished product, for example a shirt or pair of trousers. Each process that can result in either a finished good or a raw material for the next process must be evaluated separately. In such multi-process industries, process costing is used to ascertain the cost at each stage of production.
- Multiple costing or composite costing: When the output is comprised of many assembled parts or components, as with television, motor cars, or electronics gadgets, costs have to be ascertained for each component, as well as with the finished product. Such costing may involve different methods of costing for different components. Therefore, this type of costing is known as composite costing or multiple costing.
- Uniform costing: This is not a separate method of costing, but rather a system in which a number of firms in the same industry use the same method of costing, using agreed-on principles and standard accounting practices. This helps in setting the price of the product and in inter-firm comparisons.

Approaches to Cost Accounting

Different cost accounting techniques are used in different industries to analyze and present costs for the purposes of control and managerial decisions. The generally-used types of costing are as follows:

- Marginal costing: Marginal costing entails the allocation of only variable costs, i.e. direct materials, direct labour and other direct expenses, and variable overheads to the production. It does not take into account the fixed cost of production. This type of costing emphasizes the distinction between fixed and variable costs.
- Absorption costing: In absorption costing, the full costs (that is, both fixed and variable costs) are absorbed into production.
- Standard costing: In standard costing, a cost is predicted in advance of production, based on predetermined standards under a given set of operating conditions. Standard costs are compared with actual costs periodically, and revised to avoid losses due to outdated costing.
- Historical costing: Historical costing, unlike standard costing, uses actual costs, determined after they have been incurred. Almost all organizations use the historical costing system of accounting for costs.

Important Methods of Costing

Different industries adopt different methods of ascertaining costs of their products depending on the nature of the production and the type of output.

Cost sheet is the statement that shows various components of total cost of a product. It indicates per unit cost in addition to total cost. Cost sheet is prepared on the basis of historical cost and estimated cost.

Terms Associated with Costing

- Fixed cost: Fixed costs are those costs that do not vary with respect to changes in output and would accrue even if no output was produced. E.g. Rent, interest payments, property taxes and employee salaries. However, fixed costs are restricted to specific time frame, since over the long run fixed costs can vary. For example, a manufacturer may decide to expand capacity in tandem to the increase in demand for its product, requiring a higher level of expenditure on plant and equipment.
- Variable Cost: Variable cost changes proportionately to the level of output. For manufacturers, the key variable cost is the cost of materials.
- Total Cost: It is defined as the sum of fixed, variable and semi variable costs.

- Direct and Indirect cost: Direct costs typically include the major components for manufacturing goods and the labor directly required to produce those goods. Direct costs are also referred to as prime costs. On the other hand, indirect costs include plant-wide costs such as those resulting from the use of energy and fixed capital. Indirect costs are also referred to as overhead.
- Incremental cost: It is mainly the extra cost associated with manufacturing one additional unit of production. It is also referred to as differential cost.
- Opportunity Cost: It is defined as the cost of an alternative that is forgone (benefit, profit, value given up) in order to pursue a certain action.
- Sunk Cost: It is the cost that is already incurred and cannot be recovered.
- Unit costing: It is also called the single output costing. It is used in costing of products that are expressed in identical units and suitable for products that are manufactured by continuous activity.

Example: Cement Manufacturing, Dairy, Mining etc.

- Job costing: Under this method, costs are ascertained for each work order separately as each has its own specification and scope. Tailor made products also get covered by this type of costing.

Example: Repair of buildings, Painting etc.

- Contract costing: In this method costing is done for jobs that involve heavy expenditure and stretches over long period and across different sites. It is also called as terminal costing.

Example: Construction of roads and bridges, buildings etc.

- Batch costing: Through this method the costing is done for units that are produced in batches that are uniform in nature and design.

Example: Pharmaceuticals.

- Process costing: It is used for the products which go through different processes. Like in the process of manufacturing cloth, different processes are involved namely spinning, weaving and finished product. Each process gives an output that is a finished product in itself and can be sold. That is why; process costing is used to ascertain the cost of each stage of production.
- Service or operating costing: It is the method used for the costing of operating a service such as Public Bus, Railways, Nursing home. It is used to ascertain the cost of a particular service.
- Multiple costing: When the output comprises different assembled parts like in televisions, cars or electronic gadgets, cost has to be ascertained for the

component as well as the finished product. Such costing may involve different/multiple methods of costing.

- Product Costing: Product costing methods are used to assign cost to a manufactured product. The main costing methods available are process costing, job costing and direct costing. Each of these methods apply to different production and decision environments.

The main product costing methods are:

- Job costing: This is the assignment of costs to a specific manufacturing job. This method is used when individual products or batches of products are unique, and especially when jobs are being billed directly to customers or are likely to be audited by customers.
- Process costing: This is the accumulation of labor, material and overhead costs across departments or entities, with the total production cost then being allocated to individual units. Process costing is used when large quantities of the same product are manufactured, usually in long production runs.
- Inventory Costing: Different inventory costing methods are best suited to different situations and financial goals:
    - First In, First Out: Under the First In, First Out (FIFO) method, the oldest costs are assigned to inventory items sold, regardless of whether the sold items were actually purchased at that cost. When the number of inventory items purchased at the oldest cost is sold, the next oldest cost is assigned to sales.
    - Last In, First Out: The last in, first out method (LIFO) is the exact opposite of the FIFO method, assigning the most recent inventory costs to items sold.
- Average Cost Method: The average cost method assigns inventory costs by calculating a moving average of all inventory purchase costs.
- Specific Identification Method: The specific identification method perfectly matches inventory costs with units sold, assigning the exact cost of each sold inventory item when the specific item is sold.

Costing Methods for Manufacturing

Traditional Methods: Process and Job-order Costing

There are two conventional costing approaches used in manufacturing, namely process and job order costing. Process costing method analyzes the net cost of a manufacturing process. Since most manufacturing processes involve more than one step, calculation is made for each step to arrive at a unit cost average for the entire production system.

The second major costing method, job-order costing, involves costing based on an individual product basis. This is useful where each unit of production is customized or where there are very few units produced. Under this method, the exact costs incurred in the production of a particular unit are calculated and are not necessarily averaged with those of any other unit, since every unit may be different.

Activity-based Costing

Activity-based costing (ABC) is a secondary/somewhat complementary method to the two traditional costing techniques.

While traditional methods classify costs into categories like direct materials, labor and other overheads, ABC considers all the costs associated with a single manufacturing task, regardless of whether they fall under the headings of labor or materials or something else.

The benefit of this method is that management can keep track of tasks that cost the most versus which add the most value; indicating any disproportionate amount of money being spent on low-value activities, thereby indicating the need for process change.

Steps for Performing ABC

- Analyze the Activities.
- Gather all the Costs.
- Trace Costs to the Activities.
- Set up Output Measures.
- Analyze the Costs.

Features of ABC

- Indicates High Cost activities.
- Helps in establishing and monitoring performance measures.
- Is useful for forecasting financial baselines.
- Captures the current cost of performing any activity.

Activity-based Costing

Activity-based costing (ABC) is a costing method that identifies activities in an organization and assigns the cost of each activity to all products and services according to the actual consumption by each. This model assigns more indirect costs (overhead) into direct costs compared to conventional costing.

CIMA (Chartered Institute of Management Accountants) defines ABC as an approach to the costing and monitoring of activities which involves tracing resource consumptionand costing final outputs. Resources are assigned to activities, and activities to cost objects based on consumption estimates. The latter utilize cost drivers to attach activity costs to outputs.

Objectives

With ABC, a company can soundly estimate the cost elements of entire products, activities and services, that may help inform a company's decision to either:

- Identify and eliminate those products and services that are unprofitable and lower the prices of those that are overpriced (product and service portfolio aim).
- Or identify and eliminate production or service processes that are ineffective and allocate processing concepts that lead to the very same product at a better yield (process re-engineering aim).

In a business organization, the ABC methodology assigns an organization's resource costs through activities to the products and services provided to its customers. ABC is generally used as a tool for understanding product and customer cost and profitability based on the production or performing processes. As such, ABC has predominantly been used to support strategic decisions such as pricing, outsourcing, identification and measurement of process improvement initiatives.

Prevalence

Following strong initial uptake, ABC lost ground in the 1990s compared to alternative metrics, such as Kaplan's balanced scorecard and economic value added. An independent 2008 report concluded that manually driven ABC was an inefficient use of resources: it was expensive and difficult to implement for small gains, and a poor value, and that alternative methods should be used. Other reports show the broad band covered with the ABC methodology.

However, application of an activity based recording may be applied as an addition to activity based accounting, not as a replacement of any *costing* model, but to transform concurrent process accounting into a more authentic approach.

Historical Development

Traditionally, cost accountants had arbitrarily added a broad percentage of analysis into the indirect cost. In addition, activities include actions that are performed both by people and machine.

However, as the percentages of indirect or overhead costs rose, this technique became increasingly inaccurate, because indirect costs were not caused equally by all products. For example, one product might take more time in one expensive machine than another product—but since the amount of direct labor and materials might be the same, additional cost for use of the machine is not being recognized when the same broad 'on-cost' percentage is added to all products. Consequently, when multiple products share common costs, there is a danger of one product subsidizing another.

ABC is based on George Staubus' Activity Costing and Input-Output Accounting. The concepts of ABC were developed in the manufacturing sector of the United States during the 1970s and 1980s. During this time, the *Consortium for Advanced Management-International*, now known simply as *CAM-I*, provided a formative role for studying and formalizing the principles that have become more formally known as Activity-Based Costing.

Robin Cooper and Robert S. Kaplan, proponents of the Balanced Scorecard, brought notice to these concepts in a number of articles published in *Harvard Business Review* beginning in 1988. Cooper and Kaplan described ABC as an approach to solve the problems of traditional cost management systems. These traditional costing systems are often unable to determine accurately the actual costs of production and of the costs of related services. Consequently, managers were making decisions based on inaccurate data especially where there are multiple products.

Instead of using broad arbitrary percentages to allocate costs, ABC seeks to identify cause and effect relationships to objectively assign costs. Once costs of the activities have been identified, the cost of each activity is attributed to each product to the extent that the product uses the activity. In this way ABC often identifies areas of high overhead costs per unit and so directs attention to finding ways to reduce the costs or to charge more for costly products.

They initially focused on manufacturing industry where increasing technology and productivity improvements have reduced the relative proportion of the direct costs of labor and materials, but have increased relative proportion of indirect costs. For example, increased automation has reduced labor, which is a direct cost, but has increased depreciation, which is an indirect cost.

Like manufacturing industries, financial institutions have diverse products and customers, which can cause cross-product, cross-customer subsidies. Since personnel expenses represent the largest single component of non-interest expense in financial institutions, these costs must also be attributed more accurately to products and customers. Activity based costing, even though originally developed for manufacturing, may even be a more useful tool for doing this.

Activity-based costing was later explained in 1999 by Peter F. Drucker in the book *Management Challenges of the 21st Century*. He states that traditional cost accounting focuses on what it costs to *do something*, for example, to cut a screw thread; activity-based

- Training requirements: Basic training for all employees and workshop sessions for senior managers.
- Define the project scope: Evaluate mission and objectives for the project.
- Identify activities and drivers: Determine what drives what activity.
- Create a cost and operational flow diagram: How resources and activities are related to products and services.
- Collect data: Collecting data where the diagram shows operational relationship.
- Build a software model, validate and reconcile.
- Interpret results and prepare management reports.
- Integrate data collection and reporting.

Integrating EVA and Process based Costing

Recently, Mocciaro Li Destri, Picone & Minà proposed a performance and cost measurement system that integrates the economic value added (EVA) criteria with process based costing (PBC).

Authors note that activity-based costing system is introspective and focuses on a level of analysis which is too low. On the other hand, they undescore the importance to consider the cost of capital in order to bring strategy back into performance measures.

Limitations

Applicability of ABC is bound to cost of required data capture. That drives the prevalence to slow processes in services and administrations, where staff time consumed per task defines a dominant portion of cost. Hence the reported application for production tasks do not appear as a favorized scenario.

Treating Fixed Costs as Variable

The key problem with ABC, like other cost allocation approaches, is that in essence it treats fixed costs as if they were variable, thereby presenting an inaccurate picture that will lead to wrong decisions. Allocating PPE to individual products, for example, may lead to discontinuation of products that seem unprofitable after the allocation, even if in fact their discontinuation will negatively affect the bottom line.

Tracing Costs

Even in ABC, some overhead costs are difficult to assign to products and customers, such as the chief executive's salary. These costs are termed 'business sustaining' and are not assigned to products and customers because there is no meaningful method. This lump of unallocated overhead costs must nevertheless be met by contributions from each of the products, but it is not as large as the overhead costs before ABC is employed.

Although some may argue that costs untraceable to activities should be "arbitrarily allocated" to products, it is important to realize that the only purpose of ABC is to provide information to management. Therefore, there is no reason to assign any cost in an arbitrary manner.

Transition to Automated Activity-based Costing Accounting

The prerequisite for lesser cost in performing ABC is automating the data capture with an accounting extension that leads to the desired ABC model. Known approaches for event based accounting simply show the method for automation. Any transition of a current process from one stage to the next may be detected as a relevant event. Paired events easily form the respective activity.

The state of the art approach with authentication and authorization in IETF standard RADIUS gives an easy solution for accounting all workposition based activities. That simply defines the extension of the *Authentication and Authorization* (AA) concept to a more advanced *AA and Accounting* (AAA) concept. Respective approaches for AAA get defined and staffed in the context of mobile services, when using smart phones as e.a. intelligent agents or smart agents for automated capture of accounting data .

Public Sector Usage

When ABC is reportedly used in the public administration sector, the reported studies do not provide evidence about the success of methodology beyond justification of budgeting practise and existing service management and strategies.

Usage in the US Marine Corps started in 1999. Its use by the UK Police has been mandated since the 2003-04 UK tax year as part of England and Wales' National Policing Plan, specifically the Policing Performance Assessment Framework.

Activity-based Costing Method

Traditional Costing Method

In a traditional costing method, we calculate one plantwide allocation rate or we could calculate an overhead allocation rate for each department.

We have a three step pro-cess:
Step 1: Determine the basis for allocating overhead or indirect costs. These can be anything a company decides but most common are direct labor cost, direct labor hours, direct material usage or machine hours.

Step 2: Calculated a predetermined overhead rate using estimates. This is typically calculated at the end of the year to be used during the following year. The formula we use for this is:

$$\text{Predetermined Overhead Rate (POHR)} = \frac{\text{Estimated Overhead}}{\text{Estimated Base (or cost driver)}}$$

Step 3: Apply overhead throughout the period using the actual amount of our base and the predetermined overhead rate (POHR) calculated in step 2. We calculate this as:

$$\text{Applied Overhead} = \text{Actual amount of base x POHR}$$

Traditional Costing Method Example

Assume High Challenge Company makes two products, touring bicycles and mountain bicycles. The touring bicycles product line is a high-volume line, while the mountain bicycle is a low-volume, specialized product.

High Challenge Company allocated manufacturing overhead costs to the two products for the month of January. Department A had estimated overhead of $2,000,000 and used 20,000 machine hours. High Challenge has decided to allocate overhead on the basis of machine hours.

- The predetermined overhead rate of $100 per machine hour is calculated as:

$$\text{Predetermined Overhead Rate (POHR)} = \frac{\text{Estimated Overhead}}{\text{Estimated Base (or cost driver)}} \quad \frac{\$2{,}000{,}000}{20{,}000 \text{ machine hours}}$$

- At the end of January, High Challenge had used 1,500 machine hours for the Touring bicycle product line and 500 machine hours for the Mountain bicycle product line. Overhead would be allocated to each product as follows (use the POHR calculated above at $100 per machine hour):

Touring Bicycle	Mountain Bicycle
$150,000 (1,500 machine hours x $100 per hour)	$50,000 (500 machine hours x $100 per hour)

Methods used for Activity-based Costing

Activity-based costing requires accountants to use the following four steps:

- Identify the activities that consume resources and assign costs to those activities. Purchasing materials would be an activity.

- Identify the cost drivers associated with each activity. A cost driver is an activity or transaction that causes costs to be incurred. For the purchasing materials activity, the cost drivers could be the number of orders placed or the number of items ordered. Each activity could have multiple cost drivers.
- Compute a cost rate per cost driver unit. The cost driver rate could be the cost per purchase order.
- Assign costs to products by multiplying the cost driver rate times the volume of cost driver units consumed by the product. For example, the cost per purchase order times the number of orders required for Product A for the month of December would measure the cost of the purchasing activity for Product A for December.

These four steps:

Step 1, is often the most interesting and challenging part of the exercise. This step requires people to understand all of the activities required to make the product. Imagine the activities involved in making a simple product like a pizza—ordering, receiving and inspecting materials, making the dough, putting on the ingredients, baking, and so forth. Or imagine the activities involved in making a complex product such as an automobile or computer.

One of the lessons of activity-based costing has been that the more complex the business, the higher the indirect costs. Imagine that each month you produce 100,000 gallons of vanilla ice cream and your friend produces 100,000 gallons of 39 different flavors of ice cream. Further, assume your ice cream is sold only in one liter containers, while your friend sells ice cream in various containers. Your friend has more complicated ordering, storage, product testing (one of the more desirable jobs, nevertheless), and packing in containers. Your friend has more machine setups, too. Presumably, you can set the machinery to one setting to obtain the desired product quality and taste. Your friend has to set the machines each time a new flavor is produced. Although both of you produce the same total volume of ice cream, it is not hard to imagine that your friend's overhead costs would be considerably higher.

In Step 2, we identify the cost drivers. In the table below, we present several examples of the cost drivers companies use. Most cost drivers are related to either the volume of production or to the complexity of the production or marketing process.

Cost driver	Cost of assigned cost driver
Miles driven	Automobile costs
Machine-hours	Electricity to run machines
Customers served	Overhead in a bank
Flight hours	Airplane maintenance costs
Number of customers	Selling costs

In deciding which cost drivers to use, managers consider these three factors:

- Causal relation: Choosing a cost driver that causes the cost is ideal. For example, suppose students in biology classes are messier than students in history classes. As a result, the university does more maintenance per square foot in biology classrooms and labs than in history classrooms. Further, it is possible to keep track of the time maintenance people spend cleaning classrooms and labs. The university could assign maintenance costs based on the time spent in history classrooms and in biology classrooms and labs, respectively, to the history and biology departments.
- Benefits received: Choose a cost driver so costs are assigned in proportion to benefits received. For example, if the physics department in a university benefits more from the university's supercomputer than the German department does, the university should select a cost driver that recognizes such differences in benefits. The cost driver could be the number of faculty and/or students in each department who use the computer.
- Reasonableness: Some costs that cannot be linked to products based on causality or benefits received are assigned on the basis of reasonableness.

For step 3, we need to calculate the activity rates. These are calculated using the same formula for predetermined overhead rate (POHR) that we used for traditional costing. In general, predetermined rates for allocating indirect costs to products are computed as follows:

$$\text{Predetermined Overhead Rate (POHR)} = \frac{\text{Estimated Overhead}}{\text{Estimated Base (or cost driver)}}$$

This formula applies to all indirect costs, whether manufacturing overhead, administrative costs, distribution costs, selling costs, or any other indirect cost.

In Step 4, we first define the notion of an activity center. An activity center is a unit of the organization that performs some activity. For example, the costs of setting up machines would be assigned to the activity center that sets up machines. This means that each activity has associated costs. When the cost driver is the number of inspections, for example, the company must keep track of the cost of inspections.

Workers and machines perform activities on each product as it is produced. Accountants allocate costs to products by multiplying each activity's indirect cost rate by the volume of activity used in making the product. The formula we will use for each activity is:

$$\text{Applied Overhead} = \text{Actual amount of activity cost driver x activity POHR}$$

Activity-based Costing Example

Assume High Challenge Company makes two products, touring bicycles and mountain bicycles. The touring bicycles product line is a high-volume line, while the mountain bicycle is a low-volume, specialized product.

In using activity-based costing, the company identified four activities that were important cost drivers and a cost driver used to allocate overhead. These activities were (1) purchasing materials, (2) setting up machines when a new product was started, (3) inspecting products, and (4) operating machines.

Accountants estimated the overhead and the volume of events for each activity. For example, management estimated the company would purchase 100,000 pieces of materials that would require overhead costs of $200,000 for the year. These overhead costs included salaries of people to purchase, inspect, and store materials. Setting up machines for a new product would need 400 setups and overhead of $800,000. The company would have 4,000 inspections and overhead of $400,000. Finally, running machines would cost $600,000 for 20,000 machine hours.

These estimates were made last year and will be used during all of the current year. In practice, companies most frequently set rates for the entire year, although some set rates for shorter periods, such as a quarter.

Look at the overhead rates computed for the four activities in the table below. Note that the total overhead for current year is $2,000,000 using activity-based costing, just as it was using a traditional costing method. The total amount of overhead should be the same whether using activity-based costing or traditional methods of cost allocation to products. The primary difference between activity-based costing and the traditional allocation methods is the amount of detail; particularly, the number of activities used to assign overhead costs to products. Traditional allocation uses just one activity, such as machine-hours. Activity-based costing used four activities in this case. In practice, companies using activity-based costing generally use more than four activities because more than four activities are important. We used four to keep the illustration as simple as possible.

The activity cost rates (predetermined overhead rates) are calculated as follows:

Activity	Cost Driver (activity)	Overhead Cost	Estimated Units	Rate
Purchasing Materials	Pieces of materials	$ 200,000	100,000 pieces	$ 2 per piece
Machine Setups	Machine setups	800,000	400 setups	2,000 per setup
Inspections	Inspection hours	400,000	4,000 inspect. hours	100 per inspect. hour
Running Machine	Machine hours	600,000	20,000 mach. Hours	30 per machine hour
Total Overhead		$ 2,000,000		

For January, the High Challenge Company has the following information about the actual number of cost driver units for each of the two products:

	Touring	Mountain
Purchasing Materials	6,000 pieces	4,000 pieces
Machine Setups	10 setups	30 setups
Inspections	200 hours	200 hours
Running Machine	1,500 hours	1,500 hours

Multiplying the actual activity events for each product times the predetermined rates computed earlier resulted in the overhead allocated to the two products:

	Touring		Mountain	
Purchasing Materials	$ 12,000	(6,000 pieces x $2 per piece)	$ 8,000	(4,000 pieces x $2 per piece)
Machine Setups	20,000	(10 setups x $2,000 per setup)	60,000	(30 setups x $2,000 per set-up)
Inspections	20,000	(200 hours x $100 per hour)	20,000	(200 hours x $100 per hour)
Running Machine	45,000	(1,500 hours x $30 per hour)	15,000	(500 hours x $30 per hour)
Total Overhead	$ 97,000		$ 103,000	

Now we can compare the overhead allocated to the two product lines using the traditional method and activity-based costing, as follows:

	Touring bicycles	Mountain bicycles
Traditional method	$150,000	$50,000
Activity-based costing	97,000	103,000

Notice how the total overhead for the month of January is the same at $200,000 but the amount allocated to each product is different.

Analysis more overhead is allocated to the lower volume mountain bicycles using activity-based costing. The mountain bicycles are allocated more overhead per unit primarily because activity-based costing recognizes the need for more setups for mountain bicycles and for as many inspection hours for the more specialized mountain bicycles as for the higher volume touring bicycles. By failing to assign costs to all of the activities, touring bicycles were subsidizing mountain bicycles. Many companies have found themselves in similar situations. Activity-based costing has revealed that low-volume, specialized products have been the cause of greater costs than managers had realized.

Activity-based Costing with Two Activities

Let's illustrate the concept of activity based costing by looking at two common manufacturing activities: (1) the setting up of a production machine for running batches of products, and (2) the actual production of the units of product. We will assume that a company has annual manufacturing overhead costs of $2,000,000—of which $200,000 is directly involved in setting up the production machines. During the year the company expects to perform 400 machine setups. Let's also assume that the batch sizes vary considerably, but the setup efforts for each machine are similar.

The cost per setup is calculated to be $500 ($200,000 of cost per year divided by 400 setups per year). Under activity based costing, $200,000 of the overhead will be viewed as a batch-level cost. This means that $200,000 will first be allocated to batches of products to be manufactured (referred to as a Stage 1 allocation), and then be assigned to the units of product in each batch (referred to as Stage 2 allocation). For example, if Batch X consists of 5,000 units of product, the setup cost per unit is $0.10 ($500 divided by 5,000 units). If Batch Y is 50,000 units, the cost per unit for setup will be $0.01 ($500 divided by 50,000 units). For simplicity, let's assume that the remaining $1,800,000 of manufacturing overhead is caused by the production activities that correlate with the company's 100,000 machine hours.

For our simple two-activity example, let's see how the rates for allocating the manufacturing overhead would look *with* activity based costing and *without* activity based costing:

	With ABC	Without ABC
Mfg overhead coasts assigned to setups	$200,000	$-0-
Number of setups	400	Not applicable
Mfg overhead cost per setup	$500	$-0-
Total manufacturing overhead costs	$2,000,000	$2,000,000
Less: Cost traced to machine setups	200,000	-0-
Mfg O/H costs allocated on machine hours	$1,800,000	$2,000,000
Machine hours (MH)	100,000	100,000
Mfg overhead costs per MH	$18	$20
Mfg overhead cost allocation	$500 setup cost per Batch + $18 per MH	$20 per MH

Next, let's see what impact these different allocation techniques and overhead rates would have on the per unit cost of a specific unit of output. Assume that a company manufactures a batch of 5,000 units and it produces 50 units per machine hour, here is how the cost assigned to the units with activity-based costing and without activity-based costing compares:

	With ABC	Without ABC
Mfg overhead for setting up machine	$500	$-0-
No. of units in batch	5,000	Not applicable
Mfg O/H caused by Setup – Per Unit	$0.10	Not applicable
Mfg overhead costs per machine hour	$18	$20
No. of units produced per machine hour	50	50
Mfg O/H caused by Production – Per Unit	$0.36	$0.40
Total Mfg O/H Allocated – Per Unit	$0.46	$0.40

If a company manufactures a batch of 50,000 units and produces 50 units per machine hour, here is how the cost assigned to the units with ABC and without ABC compares:

	With ABC	Without ABC
Mfg overhead for setting up machine	$500	$-0-
No. of units in batch	50,000	Not applicable
Mfg O/H caused by Setup – Per Unit	$0.01	Not applicable
Mfg overhead costs per machine hour	$18	$20
No. of units produced per machine hour	50	50
Mfg O/H caused by Production – Per Unit	$0.36	$0.40
Total Mfg O/H Allocated – Per Units	$0.37	$0.40

As the tables above illustrate, with activity based costing the cost per unit decreases from $0.46 to $0.37 because the cost of the setup activity is spread over 50,000 units instead of 5,000 units. Without ABC, the cost per unit is $0.40 regardless of the number of units in each batch. If companies base their selling prices on costs, a company *not* using an ABC approach might lose the large batch work to a competitor who bids a lower price based on the lower, *more accurate* overhead cost of $0.37. It›s also possible that a company not using ABC may find itself being the low bidder for manufacturing small batches of product, since its $0.40 is lower than the ABC model of $0.46 for a batch size of 5,000 units. With its bid price based on manufacturing overhead of $0.40—but a true cost of $0.46—the company may end up doing lots of production for little or no profit.

Advantages of Activity-based Costing (ABC)

The following are the advantages of ABC:

1. Accurate Product Cost:

ABC brings accuracy and reliability in product cost determination by focusing on cause and effect relationship in the cost incurrence. It recognises that it is activities which cause costs, not products and it is product which consume activities. In advanced manufacturing environment and technology where support functions overheads constitute a large share of total costs, ABC provides more realistic product costs.

ABC produces reliable and correct product cost data in case of greater diversity among the products manufactured such as low-volume products, high-volume products. Traditional costing system is likely to bring errors and approximation in product cost determination due to using arbitrary apportionment and absorption methods.

2. Information about Cost Behaviour:

ABC identifies the real nature of cost behaviour and helps in reducing costs and identifying activities which do not add value to the product. With ABC, managers are able to control many fixed overhead costs by exercising more control over the activities which have caused these fixed overhead costs. This is possible since behaviour of many fixed overhead costs in relation to activities now become more visible and clear.

3. Tracing of Activities for the Cost Object:

ABC uses multiple cost drivers, many of which are transaction based rather than product volume. Further, ABC is concerned with all activities within and beyond the factory to trace more overheads to the products.

4. Tracing of Overhead Costs:

ABC traces costs to areas of managerial responsibility, processes, customers, departments besides the product costs.

5. Better Decision Making:

ABC improves greatly the manager's decision making as they can use more reliable product cost data. ABC helps usefully in fixing selling prices of products as more correct data of product cost is now readily available.

6. Cost Management:

ABC provides cost driver rates and information on transaction volumes which are very useful to management for cost management and performance appraisal of responsibility centres. Cost driver rates can be used advantageously for the design of new products or existing products as they indicate overhead costs that are likely to be applied in costing the product.

7. Use of Excess Capacity and Cost Reduction:

ABC, through the processes of pooling of activity costs and the identification of cost drivers, can lead to a range of applications. These include the identification of spare capacity and the fostering of cost reduction by comparing the resources required under ABC with the resources that are currently provided. This provides a platform for the development of activity-based budgeting in which the resource relationships identified by ABC are used to project future resource requirements.

8. Benefit to Service Industry:

Service organizations, such as banks, hospitals and government departments, have very different characteristics than manufacturing firms. Service organizations have almost no direct costs, most of the costs are overheads and they do not hold stocks of service as the service is consumed when it is produced. Traditional costing has generally been considered inappropriate for these organizations, whereas ABC offers the potential of benefits from improved decision making and cost management.

Disadvantages of Activity Based Costing (ABC)

The following are the demerits of ABC:

1. Expensive and Complex:

ABC has numerous cost pools and multiple cost drivers and therefore can-be more complex than traditional product costing systems. It can prove costly to manage ABC system.

2. Selection of Drivers:

Some difficulties emerge in the implementation of ABC system, such as selection of cost drivers, assignment of common costs, varying cost driver rates etc.

3. Disadvantages to Smaller Firms:

ABC has different levels of utility for different organisation such as large manufacturing firm can use it more usefully than the smaller firms. Also, it is likely that firms depending on cost-plus pricing can take advantages from ABC as it gives accurate product cost. But those firms who use market based prices may not favour ABC. The level of technology and manufacturing environment prevailing in different firms also affect the application of ABC.

4. Measurement Difficulties:

The main costs and limitations of an ABC system are the measurements necessary to implement it. ABC systems require management to estimate costs of activity pools and to identify and measure cost drivers to serve as cost allocation bases. Even basic ABC systems require many calculations to determine costs of products and services. These measurements are costly. Activity cost rates also need to be updated regularly.

Standard Cost Accounting

Standard cost accounting is a traditional cost accounting method introduced in the 1920s, as an alternative for the traditional cost accounting method based on historical costs.

Standard cost accounting uses ratios called efficiencies that compare the labor and materials actually used to produce a good with those that the same goods would have required under "standard" conditions. As long as actual and standard conditions are similar, few problems arise. Unfortunately, standard cost accounting methods developed about 100 years ago, when labor comprised the most important cost of manufactured goods. Standard methods continue to emphasize labor efficiency even though that resource now constitutes a (very) small part of the cost in most cases.

Standard cost accounting can hurt managers, workers, and firms in several ways. For example, a policy decision to increase inventory can harm a manufacturing manager's performance evaluation. Increasing inventory requires increased production, which means that processes must operate at higher rates. When (not if) something goes wrong, the process takes longer and uses more than the standard labor time. The manager appears responsible for the excess, even though s/he has no control over the production requirement or the problem.

In adverse economic times, firms use the same efficiencies to downsize, right size, or otherwise reduce their labor force. Workers laid off, under those circumstances, have even less control over excess inventory and cost efficiencies than their managers.

Many financial and cost accountants have agreed for many years on the desirability of replacing standard cost accounting. They have not, however, found a successor.

Historical Costs

Historical costs are costs whereby materials and labor may be allocated based on past experience. Historical costs are a classification of costs by time. Historical costs are costs incurred in the past. Predetermined costs are computed in advance on basis of factors affecting cost elements. In the 19th century and early 20th century time book's were used to register working time, and eventually determine historical costs.

In modern cost account of recording historical costs was taken further, by allocating the company's fixed costs over a given period of time to the items produced during that period, and recording the result as the total cost of production. This allowed the *full cost* of products that were not sold in the period they were produced to be recorded in inventory using a variety of complex accounting methods, which was consistent with the principles of Generally Accepted Accounting Principles (GAAP). It also essentially enabled managers to ignore the fixed costs, and look at the results of each period in relation to the "standard cost" for any given product.

For example: if the railway coach company normally produced 40 coaches per month, and the fixed costs were still $1000/month, then each coach could be said to incur an Operating Cost/overhead of $25 =($1000 / 40). Adding this to the variable costs of $300 per coach produced a full cost of $325 per coach.

This method tended to slightly distort the resulting unit cost, but in mass-production industries that made one product line, and where the fixed costs were relatively low, the distortion was very minor.

For example: if the railway coach company made 100 coaches one month, then the unit cost would become $310 per coach ($300 + ($1000 / 100)). If the next month the company made 50 coaches, then the unit cost = $320 per coach ($300 + ($1000 / 50)), a relatively minor difference.

Variance Analysis

An important part of standard cost accounting is a variance analysis, which breaks down the variation between actual cost and standard costs into various components (volume variation, material cost variation, labor cost variation, etc.) so managers can understand *why costs were different from what was planned* and take appropriate action to correct the situation.

Advantages and Disadvantages of Standard Costing

Advantages of Standard Costing

Management by Exception The standard costing is an example of management by exception. By studying the variances, management's attention is directed towards those items, which are not proceeding according to the plan. Most of the management's time is saved and can be directed to other value adding activities. Management only concentrates on the 'few' exceptions reported.

1. Cost Reduction: The process of setting, revising and monitoring standards encourages reappraisal of methods, materials and techniques thus leading to cost reductions. Analysis of unfavourable variances directs cost analysis to factors that are making costs to exceed the budgeted costs thus these factors can be controlled, leading to cost reduction.

2. Pricing: Standard costs serve as a reliable base of calculating total cost of producing a good or service, to which a margin can be added to determine the selling price.

3. Inventory Valuation: Standard costing makes inventory valuation much easier, if the actual number of physical units in the inventory is known, then the inventory value is simply determined by multiplying the standard cot per unit by the physical units.

4. Motivation: A properly developed standard costing system requires the full participation of all management levels (upper, middle and lower levels) and the employees. This creates motivation for the employees as they feel part of the system.

5. Cost Control: A well implemented standard costing system acts as a yardstick against which all costs are measured to determine whether the variance from the standard is favourable or unfavourable. This creates cost consciousness in the organization and in the end enables the organization to control costs.

6. Budgeting is made easier One of the greatest benefits of standard costing is to be found in setting budgets for the organization and its departments. As earlier illustrated once the desired output units are known, then the budgeted cost is simply the output units desired multiplied by the standard cost per unit i.e. Budgeted Cost = Output units x Standard Cost per unit.

7. Performance Evaluation is Simplified As already noted, standard costing creates a cost consciousness in the organization so that any cost can be easily evaluated whether it has favourable or unfavourable variance, so that appropriate corrective measures can be taken. Once budgets are prepared and agreed upon (anticipatively), and employees performance can be acceptably measure against the set standards to determine whether the performance is acceptable or not: appropriate corrective measures (punishment or reward) can then be acceptably taken by the management.

Disadvantages of Standard Costing

1. The system of standard costing is expensive to install A lot of money is spent in studying output requirements in terms of labour, materials and overheads.

2. Time Consuming A lot of time is also spent in developing and installing reliable standard costing systems.

3. Obsolescence: In fast changing conditions (e.g. in hyperinflationary economies where prices of labour, materials and overheads change rapidly), standards become out of date quickly. They therefore lose their control and motivational effects.

4. Hard to Understand Some standard costing systems are overly elaborate and are therefore not well understood by line managers and employees. This makes their implementation difficult.

5. Effectiveness depends on Environment For standard costing systems to be effective in cost control and performance evaluation, then a participative and democratic management style is required. The top management and employees need to be committed to attaining the set standards of performance. An effective and efficient management information system is also required so as to provide employees and managers with reliable, accurate and timely feedback regarding their performance. Lack of one or more of these requirements frustrates the success of a standard costing system so that its effectiveness cannot be realized.

6. It is Subjective As we have already seen, there are several types of standards that an organization can adopt (basic, ideal, attainable and cement). What is therefore a standard in an organization depends on its management. It is also important to note that what is referred to as a significant variance depends on the organization's management, thus the subjectivity. If this subjectivity is poorly managed, (for example, punishing employees for insignificant

unfavourable variances of for variances arising from factors beyond their control), then a standard costing system can lead to employee frustration and poor goal con-gruence in the organization.

Marginal Costing

Marginal Costing is a costing technique wherein the marginal cost, i.e. variable cost is charged to units of cost, while the fixed cost for the period is completely written off against the contribution.

The term marginal cost implies the additional cost involved in producing an extra unit of output, which can be reckoned by total variable cost assigned to one unit. It can be calculated as:

Marginal Cost = Direct Material + Direct Labor + Direct Expenses + Variable Overheads

Characteristics of Marginal Costing

- Classification into Fixed and Variable Cost: Costs are bifurcated, on the basis of variability into fixed cost and variable costs. In the same way, semi variable cost is separated.
- Valuation of Stock: While valuing the finished goods and work in progress, only variable cost are taken into account. However, the variable selling and distribution overheads are not included in the valuation of inventory.
- Determination of Price: The prices are determined on the basis of marginal cost and marginal contribution.
- Profitability: The ascertainment of departmental and product's profitability is based on the contribution margin.

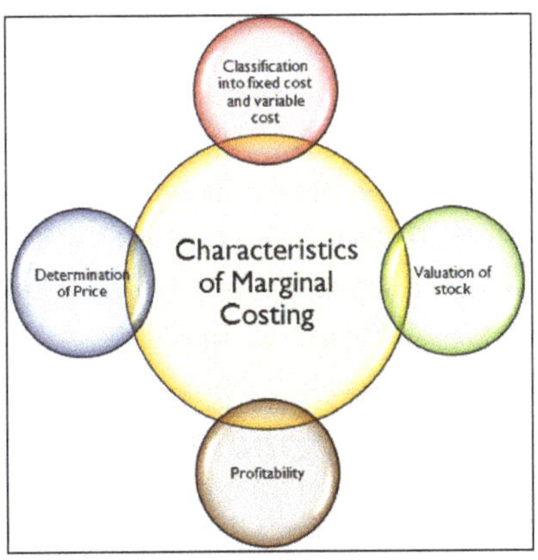

In addition to the characteristics, marginal costing system brings together the techniques of cost recording and reporting.

Marginal Costing Approach

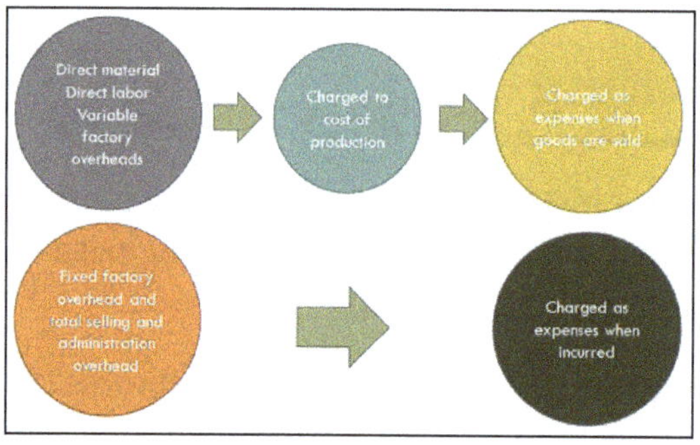

The difference between product costs and period costs forms a basis for marginal costing technique, wherein only variable cost is considered as the product cost while the fixed cost is deemed as a period cost, which incurs during the period, irrespective of the level of activity.

Facts Concerning Marginal Costing

- Cost Ascertainment: The basis for ascertaining cost in marginal costing is the nature of cost, which gives an idea of the cost behavior, that has a great impact on the profitability of the firm.
- Special technique: It is not a unique method of costing, like contract costing, process costing, batch costing. But, marginal costing is a different type of technique, used by the managers for the purpose of decision making. It provides a basis for understanding cost data so as to gauge the profitability of various products, processes and cost centers.
- Decision Making: It has a great role to play, in the field of decision making, as the changes in the level of activity pose a serious problem to the management of the undertaking.

Marginal Costing assists the managers in taking end number of business decisions, such as replacement of machines, discontinuing a product or service, etc. It also helps the management in ascertaining the appropriate level of activity, through break even analysis, that reflect the impact of increasing or decreasing production level, on the company's overall profit.

Advantages and Benefits of Marginal Costing

- Cost control: Marginal costing makes it easier to determine and control costs of production. By avoiding the arbitrary allocation of fixed overhead costs, management can concentrate on achieving and maintaining a uniform and consistent marginal cost.

- Simplicity: Marginal costing is simple to understand and operate and it can be combined with other forms of costing (e.g. budgetary costing and standard costing) without much difficulty.
- Elimination of cost variance per unit: Since fixed overheads are not charged to the cost of production in marginal costing, units have a standard cost.
- Short-term profit planning: Marginal costing can help in short-term profit planning and is easily demonstrated with break-even charts and profit graphs. Comparative profitability can be easily assessed and brought to the notice of the management for decision-making.
- Accurate overhead recovery rate: This method of costing eliminates large balances left in overhead control accounts, which makes it easier to ascertain an accurate overhead recovery rate.
- Maximum return to the business: With marginal costing, the effects of alternative sales or production policies are more readily appreciated and assessed, ensuring that the decisions taken will yield the maximum return to the business.

Disadvantages and Limitations of Marginal Costing

- Classifying costs: It is very difficult to separate all costs into fixed and variable costs clearly, since all costs are variable in the long run. Hence such classification sometimes may give misleading results. Furthermore, in a firm with many different kinds of products, marginal costing can prove less useful.
- Accurately representing profits: Since the closing stock consists only of variable costs and ignores fixed costs (which could be considerable), this gives a distorted picture of profits to shareholders.
- Semi-variable costs: Semi-variable costs are either excluded or incorrectly analyzed, leading to distortions.
- Recovery of overheads: With marginal costing, there is often the problem of under or over-recovery of overheads, since variable costs are apportioned on an estimated basis and not on actual value.
- External reporting: Marginal costing cannot be used in external reports, which must have a complete view of all indirect and overhead costs.
- Increasing costs: Since it is based on historical data, marginal costing can give an inaccurate picture in the presence of increasing costs or increasing production.

Lean Accounting

Lean accounting is the collection of principles and processes that provide numerical feedback for manufacturers implementing lean manufacturing and lean inventory practices. When you make changes to operations, such as organizing processes in different ways or shifting the ways you use your workers' time, it may be difficult to tell from simply observing workflow how much of a difference these adjustments have made. Production may seem smoother and easier and customers may seem more satisfied, but quantifying these results provides relevant, high-quality information, allowing managers to actually see the consequences of different approaches to workflow and to compare results. The information you receive from lean accounting can provide the basis for making further changes and adjustments, which your lean accounting system can also measure and evaluate.

Lean accounting treats some traditional accounting principles in nontraditional ways because conventional accounting protocols don't fully reflect the value that comes from a lean manufacturing approach. For example, traditional accounting treats inventory as an asset because it quantifies something you own rather than something you owe. Your business might manufacture parts that it later uses in finished products that are sold to customers. If you focus manufacturing resources on producing a large quantity of a particular part, your traditional balance sheet will record the inventory you've produced as an asset which increases your net worth even if it just sits on the shelf of your warehouse for a year. Lean accounting, however, takes into account the fact that unused inventory can actually be detrimental to the well being of your business because it takes up space and requires labor and materials expenditures that you could be using instead to fill a more current order.

Concepts of Lean Manufacturing

The concepts of lean manufacturing revolve around paring down manufacturing and inventory to streamline your operations toward filling current orders with as little turnaround time as possible. This approach redefines efficiency, focusing on throughput (completing and delivering finished products to customers who have placed orders). Traditional accounting instead measures efficiency in terms of how many units your production line completes, regardless of whether customers have placed orders for these units.

A traditional accounting system might show impressive numbers by virtue of the fact that you've leveraged economies of scale and made large quantities of a particular part. These traditional metrics focus on the average amount of time and labor you expend in the process of making each unit without considering the bigger picture. For example, your business will experience a different financial outcome if you deliver parts to an eager customer who will pay for them immediately rather than storing these parts in your warehouse in anticipation of future orders.

Lean manufacturing also emphasizes the principle of short turnaround time. If your business focuses on filling orders as you receive them rather than building up large quantities of particular parts, you'll end up with less waste because the parts you've manufactured in quantity may not be the parts you actually need once the orders start rolling in. Lean accounting quantifies these savings, measuring results in terms of sales relative to inventory and the lead time between a customer placing an order and your company filling and delivering it.

Communication and feedback systems are key in lean manufacturing. The sooner your warehouse and manufacturing teams know what orders have been placed, the sooner they can order the materials they need and set production processes in motion. The lean inventory approach depends on lining up suppliers who can get you what you need as quickly as possible after an order has been placed.

What are the Five "S" in Kaizen?

Kaizen is another important lean manufacturing principle based on a Japanese operations philosophy that emphasizes continual improvement. Kaizen can be summarized in five principles that all start with the letter "s".

1. Sort: With its strong emphasis on keeping inventory levels to a minimum, lean manufacturing relies on the Kaizen principle of sorting, or identifying items that are no longer useful and getting them out of the way. This practice eliminates clutter and cuts down on the time your team has to spend cataloging and rotating stock that may not even be used. Lean accounting measures the time you save here by evaluating the efficiency of your systems overall once you've gotten unnecessary stock out of the way.

2. Set in order: Once you've identified which inventory items you'll keep versus those you'll discard, the Kaizen approach emphasizes creating order among the stock you still have on hand. The process of organizing seems on the surface to interfere with productivity because you're spending time arranging rather than producing. However, lean accounting's observations demonstrate that spending this extra time actually saves time in the long run because you don't spend unnecessary hours looking for what you need in a chaotic warehouse.

3. Shine: Like setting items in order, keeping your work space clean makes the most of your resources by allowing your business to operate smoothly and without clutter, unnecessary accidents or equipment malfunctions due to improper care. The net gains from this extra care show up in your lean accounting numbers in the form of increased efficiency and lower repair bills.

4. Standardize: Every manufacturing operation has elements in common with other operations and elements that are unique to its specifications and processes. Lean manufacturing identifies and standardizes best practices, drawing on general industry knowledge and also proprietary information developed by your staff. By assembling

these insights into operations manuals and training staff effectively, you'll lower labor costs by minimizing mistakes and maximizing efficiency. You'll also increase customer satisfaction through increased consistency. Your lean accounting system will capture these improvements with data that shows strong sales and efficient use of labor hours.

5. Sustain: Once you've put the necessary energy and resources into the first four stages of the Kaizen process, you must also develop systems and sensibilities that encourage your staff to sustain and maintain the improvements they've made and even continue improving on them. Lean accounting can track your ability to sustain these efforts by following your progress over time and spotting emerging problems if your systems start to slip.

Lean Accounting Reports

Although your business may successfully and passionately implement lean manufacturing and lean inventory practices, the success of these practices are not always reflected in traditional accounting reports. The effect of lean inventory on your balance sheet is the most striking example of this discrepancy: Lower inventory levels keep your business running smoothly and profitably, but they show up on a traditional balance sheet as a variable that causes your company to have less value, at least on paper. However, if you're using lean principles successfully, this hit to your balance sheet will be balanced by a corresponding increase in the bottom line of your profit and loss statement, which over time will bounce back to your balance sheet as more cash in the bank.

If you're applying for a loan from a banker who isn't versed in lean principles, you may have to explain these concepts. You can provide notes to accompany your financial statements, or you can provide explanations in person at face-to-face meetings. This background information will help to flesh out your loan application and will provide an opportunity for you to create a well-rounded impression and appeal to the lender's discretion. It is generally a good idea to reach out to lenders and start developing relationships before you get to the point of submitting an application for financing. This relationship-building is especially important if your business works with concepts and approaches such as lean manufacturing, which may be unfamiliar to the lender.

Lean manufacturing and inventory show up on a pro forma cash-flow statement in the form of lower expenses that result in a less-urgent need for outside operating capital, reflecting a lean approach to finance. If you shorten lead times for producing and delivering orders and you keep less inventory on hand, the cash flow needs on your pro forma (and in your actual operations) will sync more closely with incoming cash. Instead of investing in a glut of inventory that requires a large payment up front but brings in revenue over an extended period of time, a lean operation spends money as closely as possible to when it delivers orders and bills customers.

A business using lean manufacturing practices can also develop customized accounting reports that measure its success using lean parameters. For example, you might track the flow of parts and labor over time to glean information about how smoothly and effectively your operations are flowing, or you might compile regular reports that measure inventory turnover, a critical variable in keeping your systems tight and lean.

Lean Accounting Practices

In addition to tracking the success of lean practices on the manufacturing floor, lean accounting should itself be lean. Its processes should be streamlined and should not require more effort and resources than necessary. To transition to a lean accounting system, it's helpful to use a system that mirrors the five "s" approach of Kaizen. First, sort your accounting operations, evaluating them with an eye toward determining which steps provide the most value relative to the time they take. Discard processes that aren't necessary for legal accounting requirements. Also eliminate steps and reports that don't give quality information about how well your lean systems are working.

After sorting your processes, set them in order by developing a sequence of tasks that makes the most of your accounting time and also yields the best possible information. For example, when evaluating workflow it makes sense to track inventory purchases before recording sales figures because the inventory is necessary to generate the sales rather than vice versa. Next, shine your processes by eliminating unnecessary steps and upgrading your spreadsheets and platforms so they'll provide the best-quality information with the least amount of input and backtracking.

Once your systems have been tightened and cleaned, start standardizing your lean accounting processes by creating written protocols and training personnel to follow these clear procedures accurately and consistently. Create standards and schedules for recording information and relaying it to coworkers who rely on these figures to understand and evaluate their production and purchasing activities.

Finally, sustain your lean accounting practices by following through and doing the scheduled tasks on schedule and making sure your coworkers do the same. Evaluate these processes regularly and update them as often as necessary, especially as systems and circumstances evolve. Keep accounting and production staff informed about changes you've implemented, especially when these changes affect their work and their responsibilities.

Target Costing

Target costing is an approach to determine a product's life-cycle cost which should be sufficient to develop specified functionality and quality, while ensuring its desired profit. It involves setting a target cost by subtracting a desired profit margin from a competitive market price. A target cost is the maximum amount of cost that can be incurred on a product, however, the firm can still earn the required profit margin from that product at a particular selling price. Target costing decomposes the target cost from product level to component level. Through this decomposition, target costing spreads the competitive pressure faced by the company to product's designers and suppliers. Target costing consists of cost planning in the design phase of production as well as cost control throughout the resulting product life cycle. The cardinal rule of target costing is to never exceed the target cost. However, the focus of target costing is not to minimize costs, but to achieve a desired level of cost reduction determined by the target costing process.

Process of Target Costing

The process of target costing can be divided into three parts: the first part involves in market-driven target costing, which focuses on studying market conditions to identify a product's allowable cost in order to meet the company's long-term profit at expected selling price; the second part involves performing cost reduction strategies with the product designer's effort and creativity to identify the product-level target cost; the third part is component-level target cost which decomposes the production cost to functional and component levels to transmit cost responsibility to suppliers.

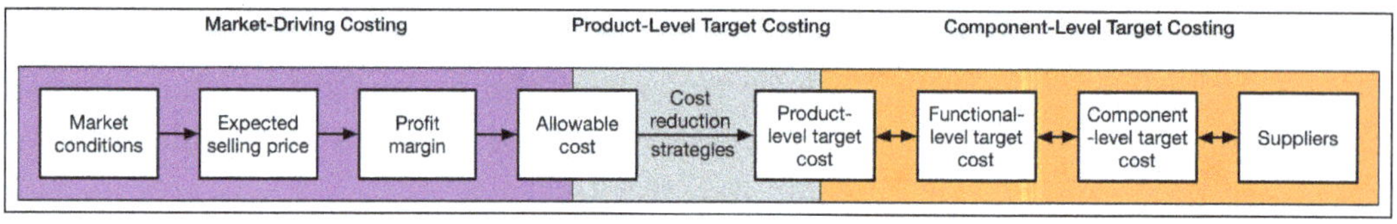

Target costing process

Market-driven Target Costing

Market driven target costing is the first part in the target costing process which focuses on studying market conditions and determining the company's profit margin in order to identify the allowable cost of a product. Market driven costing can go through 5 steps including: establish company's long-term sales and profit objective; develop the mix of products; identify target selling price for each product; identify profit margin for each product; and calculate allowable cost of each product.

Company's long-term sales and profit objectives are developed from an extensive analysis of relevant information relating to customers, market and products. Only realistic plans are accepted to proceed to the next step. Product mix is designed carefully to ensure that it satisfies many customers, but also does not contain too many products to confuse customers. Company may use simulation to explore the impact of overall profit objective to different product mixes and determine the most feasible product mix. Target selling price, target profit margin and allowable cost are identified for each product. Target selling price need to consider to the expected market condition at the time launching the product. Internal factors such as product's functionality and profit objective, and external factors such as company's image or expected price of competitive products will influence target selling price. Company's long-term profit plan and life-cycle cost are considered when determining target profit margin. Firms might set up target profit margin based on either actual profit margin of previous products or target profit margin of product line. Simulation for overall group profitability can help to make sure achieving group target. Subtracting target profit margin from target selling price results in allowable cost for each product. Allowable cost is the cost that can spend on the product to ensure meeting profit target if selling it at target price. It is the signal about the magnitude of cost saving that team need to achieve.

Product-level Target Costing

Following the completion of market-driven costing, the next task of the target costing process is product-level target costing. Product-level target costing concentrates on designing products that satisfy the company's customers at the allowable cost. To achieve this goal, product-level target costing is typically divided into three steps as shown below.

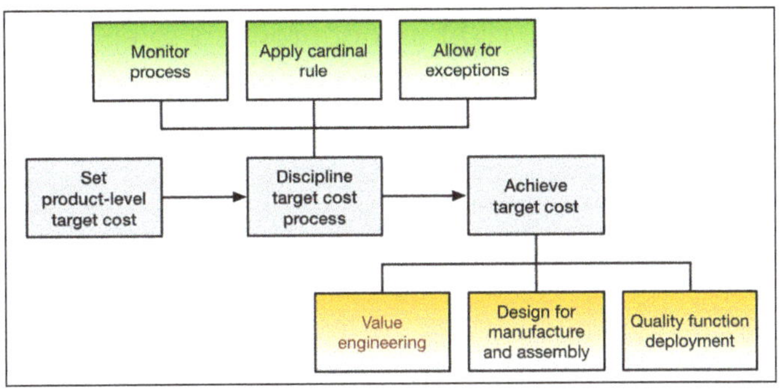

Product-level target costing

The first step is to set a product-level target cost. Since the allowable cost is simply obtained from external conditions without considering the design capabilities of the company as well as the realistic cost for manufacturing, it may not be always achievable in practice. Thus, it is necessary to adjust the unachievable allowable cost to an achievable target cost that the cost increase should be reduced with great effort. The second step is to discipline this target cost process, including monitoring the relationship between the target cost and the estimated product cost at any point during the design process, applying the cardinal rule so that the total target costs at the component-level does not exceed the target cost of the product, and allowing exceptions for products violating the cardinal rule. For a product exception to the cardinal rule, two analyses are often performed after the launch of the product. One involves reviewing the design process to find out why the target cost was unachieved. The other is an immediate effort to reduce the excessive cost to ensure that the period of violation is as short as possible. Once the target cost-reduction objective is identified, the product-level target costing comes to the final step, finding ways to achieve it. Engineering methods such as value engineering (VE), design for manufacture and assembly (DFMA), and quality function deployment (QFD) are commonly adopted in this step.

Target Costing and Value Engineering

Value engineering (VE), also known as value analysis (VA), plays a crucial role in the target costing process, particularly at the product level and the component level. Among the three aforementioned methods in achieving the target cost, VE is the most critical one because not only does it attempt to reduce costs, but also aims to improve the functionality and quality of products. There are a variety of practical VE strategies, including zero-look, first-look and second-look VE approaches, as well as teardown approaches.

Regarding the complexity of problems in the real world, implementing the target costing process often relies on the computer simulation to reproduce stochastic elements. For example, many firms use simulation to study the complex relationship between selling prices and profit margins, the impact of individual product decisions on overall group profitability, the right mix of products to enhance overall profit, or other economic modeling to overcome organizational inertia by getting the most productive reasoning. In addition, simulation helps estimate results rapidly for dynamic process changes.

Factors Affecting Target Costing

The factors influencing the target costing process is broadly categorized based on how a company's strategy for a product's quality, functionality and price change over time. However, some factors play a specific role based on what drives a company's approach to target costing.

Factors Influencing Market-driven Costing

Intensity of competition and nature of the customer affect market-driven costing. Competitors introducing similar products has been shown to drive rival companies to expend energy on implementing target costing systems such as in the case of Toyota and Nissan or Apple and Google. The costing process is also affected by the level of customer sophistication, changing requirements and the degree to which their future requirements are known. The automotive and camera industry are prime examples for how customers affect target costing based on their exact requirements.

Factors Influencing Product-level Costing

Product strategy and product characteristics affect product-level target costing. Characteristics of product strategy such as number of products in line, rate of redesign operations and level of innovation are shown to have an effect. Higher number of products has a direct correlation with the benefits of target costing. Frequent redesigns lead to the introduction of new products that have created better benefits to target costing. It has to be noted that the value of historical information reduces with greater innovation, thereby, reducing the benefits of product level target costing.

The degree of complexity of the product, level of investments required and the duration of product development process make up the factors that affect the target costing process based on product characteristics. Product viability is determined by the aforementioned factors. In turn, the target costing process is also modified to suit the different degrees of complexity required.

Factors Influencing Component-level Costing

Supplier-Base strategy is the main factor that determines component-level target costing because it is known to play a key role in the details a firm has about its supplier capabilities. There are three characteristics that make up the supplier-base strategy, including the degree of horizontal integration, power over suppliers and nature of supplier relations. Horizontal integration captures the fraction of product costs sourced externally. Cost pressures on suppliers can drive target costing if the buying power of firms is high enough. In turn, this may lead to better benefits. More cooperative supplier relations have been shown to increase mutual benefits in terms of target costs particularly at a component level.

Applications

Aside from the application of target costing in the field of manufacturing, target costing are also widely used in the following areas.

Energy

An Energy Retrofit Loan Analysis Model has been developed using a Monte Carlo (MC) method for target costing in Energy Efficient buildings and construction. MC method has been shown to be effective in determining the impact of financial uncertainties in project performance.

Target Value Design Decision Making Process (TVD-DMP) groups a set of energy efficiency methods at different optimization levels to evaluate costs and uncertainties involved in the energy efficiency process. Some major design parameters are specified using this methods including Facility Operation Schedule, Orientation, Plug load, HVAC and lighting systems.

The entire process consists of three phases: initiation, definition and alignment. Initiation stage involves developing a business case for energy efficiency using target value design (TVD) training, organization and compensation. The definition process involves defining and validating the case by tools such as values analysis and bench marking processes to determine the allowable costs. By setting targets and designing the design process to align with those targets, TVD-DMP has been shown to achieve a high level of collaboration needed for energy efficiency investments. This is done by using risk analysis tools, pull planning and rapid estimating processes.

Healthcare

Target costing and target value design have applications in building healthcare facilities including critical components such as Neonatal Intensive Care Units (NICUs). The process is influenced by unit locations, degree of comfort, number of patients per room, type of supply location and access to nature. According to National Vital Statistics Reports, 12.18% of 2009 births were premature and the cost per infant was $51,600. This led to opportunities for NICUs to implement target value design for deciding whether to build a single-family room or more open-bay NICUs. This was achieved using set-based design analysis which challenges the designer to generate multiple alternatives for the same functionality. Designs are evaluated keeping in mind the requirements of the various stakeholders in the NICU including nurses, doctors, family members and administrators. Unlike linear point-based design, set-based design narrows options to the optimal one by eliminating alternatives simultaneously defined by user constraints.

Construction

About 15% construction project in Japan adopted target costing for their cost planning and management as recognized by Jacomit. In the U.S., target costing research has been carried out within the framework of lean construction as target value design (TVD) method and have been disseminated widely over construction industry in recent years. Research has proven that if being applied systematically, TVD can deliver a significant improvement in project performance with average reduction of 15% in comparison with market cost. TVD in construction project considers the final cost of project as a design parameter, similar to the capacity and aesthetics requirements for the project. TVD requires the project team to develop a target cost from the beginning. The project team is expected not to design exceeding the target cost without the owner's approval, and must use different skills to maintain this target cost. In some cases, the cost can increase but the project team must commit to decrease and must try their best to decrease without impacting on other functions of the project.

Life-cycle Cost

Whole-life cost refers to the total cost of ownership over the life of an asset. The concept is also known as "Life-cycle cost" (LCC) or Lifetime cost, and is commonly referred to as "cradle to grave" or "womb to tomb" costs. Costs considered include the financial cost which is relatively simple to calculate and also the environmental and social costs which are more difficult to quantify and assign numerical values. Typical areas of expenditure which are included in calculating the whole-life cost include planning, design, construction and acquisition, operations, maintenance, renewal and rehabilitation, depreciation and cost of finance and replacement or disposal.

Financial

Whole-life cost analysis is often used for option evaluation when procuring new assets and for decision-making to minimize whole-life costs throughout the life of an asset. It is also applied to comparisons of actual costs for similar asset types and as feedback into future design and acquisition decisions.

The primary benefit is that costs which occur after an asset has been constructed or acquired, such as maintenance, operation, disposal, become an important consideration in decision-making. Previously, the focus has been on the up-front capital costs of creation or acquisition, and organisations may have failed to take account of the longer-term costs of an asset. It also allows an analysis of business function interrelationships. Low development costs may lead to high maintenance or customer service costs in the future. When making this calculation, the depreciation cost on the capital expense should not be included.

Environmental and Social

The use of environmental costs in a whole-life analysis allows a true comparison options, especially where both are quoted as "good" for the environment. For a major project such as the construction of a nuclear power station it is possible to calculate the environmental impact of making the concrete containment, the water required for refining the copper for the power plants and all the other components. Only by undertaking such an analysis is it possible to determine whether one solution carries a lower or higher environmental cost than another.

Almost all major projects have some social impact. This may be the compulsory re-location of people living on land about to be submerged under a reservoir or a threat to the livelihood of small traders from the development of a hypermarket nearby.

Whole-life Cost Topics

Project Appraisal

Whole-life costing is a key component in the economic appraisal associated with evaluating asset acquisition proposals. An economic appraisal is generally a broader based assessment, considering benefits and indirect or intangible costs as well as direct costs.

In this way, the whole-life costs and benefits of each option are considered and usually converted using discount rates into net present value costs and benefits. This results in a benefit cost ratio for each option, usually compared to the "do-nothing" counterfactual. Typically the highest benefit-cost ratio option is chosen as the preferred option.

Historically, asset investments have been based on expedient design and lowest cost construction. If such investment has been made without proper analysis of the standard of service required and the maintenance and intervention options available, the initial saving may result in increased expenditure throughout the asset's life.

By using whole-life costs, this avoids issues with decisions being made based on the short-term costs of design and construction. Often the longer-term maintenance and operation costs can be a significant proportion of the whole-life cost.

Asset Management

During the life of the asset, decisions about how to maintain and operate the asset need to be taken in context with the effect these activities might have on the residual life of the asset. If by investing 10% more per annum in maintenance costs the asset life can be doubled, this might be a worthwhile investment.

Other issues which influence the lifecycle costs of an asset include:

- Site Conditions,
- Historic performance of assets or materials,
- Effective monitoring techniques,
- Appropriate intervention strategies.

Although the general approach to determining whole-life costs is common to most types of asset, each asset will have specific issues to be considered and the detail of the assessment needs to be tailored to the importance and value of the asset. High cost assets (and asset systems) will likely have more detail, as will critical assets and asset systems.

Maintenance expenditure can account for many times the initial cost of the asset. Although an asset may be constructed with a design life of 30 years, in reality it will possibly perform well beyond this design life. For assets like these a balanced view between maintenance strategies and renewal/rehabilitation is required. The appropriateness of the maintenance strategy must be questioned, the point of intervention for renewal must be challenged. The process requires proactive assessment which must be based on the performance expected of the asset, the consequences and probabilities of failures occurring, and the level of expenditure in maintenance to keep the service available and to avert disaster.

IT Industry Usage

Whole-life cost is often referred to as "total cost of ownership (TCO)" when applied to IT hardware and software acquisitions. Use of the term "TCO" appears to have been popularised by Gartner Group in 1987 but its roots are considerably older, dating at least to the first quarter of the twentieth century.

It has since been developed as a concept with a number of different methodologies and software tools. A TCO assessment ideally offers a final statement reflecting not only the cost of purchase but all aspects in the further use and maintenance of the equipment, device, or system considered. This includes the costs of training support personnel and the users of the system, costs associated with failure or outage (planned and unplanned), diminished performance incidents (i.e. if users are kept waiting), costs of security breaches (in loss of reputation and recovery costs), costs of disaster preparedness and recovery, floor space, electricity, development expenses, testing infrastructure and expenses, quality assurance, boot image control, marginal incremental growth, decommissioning, e-waste handling, and more. When incorporated in any financial benefit analysis (e.g., ROI, IRR, EVA, ROIT, RJE) TCO provides a cost basis for determining the economic value of that investment.

Understanding and familiarity with the term TCO has been somewhat facilitated as a result of various comparisons between the TCO of open source and proprietary software. Because the software cost of open source software is often zero, TCO has been used as a means to justify the up-front licensing costs of proprietary software. Studies which attempt to establish the TCO and provide comparisons have as a result been the subject of many discussions regarding the accuracy or perceived bias in the comparison.

Automobile Industry and Finances

Total cost of ownership is also common in the automobile industry. In this context, the TCO denotes the cost of owning a vehicle from the purchase, through its maintenance, and finally its sale as a used car. Comparative TCO studies between various models help consumers choose a car to fit their needs and budget.

TCO can and often does vary dramatically against TCA (total cost of acquisition), although TCO is far more relevant in determining the viability of any capital investment, especially with modern credit markets and financing. TCO also directly relates to a business's total costs across all projects and processes and, thus, its profitability. Some instances of "TCO" appear to refer to "total cost of operation", but this may be a subset of the total cost of ownership if it excludes maintenance and support costs.

Project Accounting

Project accounting is a specialised form of accounting that corresponds to the ever-evolving needs of project delivery, which helps adequately track, report and analyse financial results and implications. This includes the practice of creating financial reports specifically designed to track the financial progress of projects, which can then be used by managers to aid project management.

Traditionally, project accounting and its principles were largely used to track and report predominantly large construction, engineering and government projects. Today, project management delivery methodologies have expanded into several other sectors, including financial, technology and legal. Subsequently, project accounting has needed to follow to cover these areas to ensure corresponding financial tracking and financial implications are understood and considered.

The need for project accounting arose as a specialised field from the nature of projects being treated as separate temporary individualised entities set up for the purpose of delivering one or more business products. As the nature of each project may be different to the business-as-usual activities run by the business; existent management accounting and financial accounting skills were recognised as insufficient to accurately advise on the treatment and financial reporting of a project. Hence, a new field emerged within the accounting sphere project accounting.

Project accounting therefore includes:

- A separate accounting system or cost centre to track and report project specific transactions, with project revenues, costs, assets and liabilities identified and allocated to the project.
- Frequent reporting, with the frequency often increasing as the project approaches completion.
- A layer of simplified reporting, including key performance indicators relevant to whether the project is on or off track. For instance traffic lights on a dashboard.
- A process for identifying project related transactions in the main accounting system and allocating or apportioning these to the project accounting system.
- Forecasting of costs to complete the project. Key stakeholders are often not only focused on the costs incurred to date, but also those committed and the expected final cost.

Projects differ to the day-to-day business-as-usual (BAU) activities in that they frequently cross organisational boundaries, may last for anything from a few days or weeks to a number of years, during which time budgets may also be revised many times. They may also be one of a number of projects that make up a larger overall project or program.

Consequently, in a project management environment costs (both direct and overhead) and revenues are also allocated to projects, which may be subdivided into a work breakdown structure, and grouped together into project hierarchies. Project accounting permits reporting at any such level that has been defined, and often allows comparison with historical as well as current budgets.

Project accounting is commonly used by government contractors, where the ability to account for costs by contract (and sometimes contract line item, or CLIN) is usually a requirement for interim payments.

Percentage-of-completion is frequently independently assessed by a project manager, program management officer (PMO) and project accountant. It includes the continuous recognition of revenues and income related to longer-term projects. By doing this, the seller is able to identify some gain or loss relevant to a project in every accounting period that is ongoing active. Funding advances and actual-to-budget cost variances are calculated using the project budget adjusted to percent-of-completion.

Where labor costs are a significant portion of overall project cost, it is usually necessary for employees to fill out a timesheet in order to generate the data to allocate project costs.

The capital budget processes of corporations and governments are chiefly concerned with major investment projects that typically have upfront costs and longer term benefits. Investment go/no-go decisions are largely based on net present value assessments. Project accounting of the costs and benefits can provide crucially important feedback on the quality of these important decisions.

An interesting specialised form of project accounting is production accounting, which tracks the costs of individual movie and television episode film production costs. A movie studio will employ production accounting to track the costs of its many separate projects.

Percentage of Completion Method

The percentage-of-completion method permits companies to record profits as development is made toward the finishing of the project. This method is not to be used when compelling uncertainty's about the percentage of completion of the remaining costs to be incurred. The method instead works at its finest when it is rationally likely to estimate the stages of the project in process.

The percentage-of-completion may be measured in any of the resulting ways:

- Cost-to-cost method: This is an example of the contract cost acquired to date the total expected cost. The price of the products already bought for a contract however have not yet been installed should not be added in the perseverance of the percentage of completion of a project, not unless they were particularly created for the contract. Also, assign the cost of equipment over the contract course, rather than direct, unless title to the supplies is being transported to the customer.
- Efforts-expended method: This is the share of effort consumed to date in comparison to the total effort expected for the agreement. E.g. the percentage of

completion may possibly be established on direct work hours, machine hours, or material size.

- Units-of-delivery-method: This is the portion of units delivered to the buyer to the overall number of units to be brought under the terms of a contract. It should only be in use when the builder produces a number of units to the requirements of a buyer. The recognition is established on:
  - For revenue, the contract price of units delivered.
  - For expenses, the costs reasonably allocable to the units delivered.

However, the necessary steps are the following:

- Subtract the total predicted contract costs from total approximated revenues to appear at the total estimated gross margin.
- Measure the range of process toward completion, using one of the methods mentioned.
- Increase the total likely contract revenue by the estimated finishing percentage to arrive at the total amount of revenue that can be acknowledged.
- Subtract the contract revenue allowed to date through the foregoing period from the complete amount of revenue that be accepted. Recognise the development in the current accounting period.
- Consider the cost of the received revenue in the same manner. This means raising the same percentage of completion by the total supposed contract cost, and subtracting the amount formerly realised to arrive at the cost of collected revenue to be recognised in the current accounting period.

Calculations

The following calculation is used to determine the completion percentage:

Percent Complete = Cost Incurred to Date / Total Cost Estimate

The current period revenue to be recognised during production would then be:

Current Period Revenue = (Percent Complete x Total Contract Revenue) - Revenue Recognised in Prior Periods

Production Accounting

Production Accounting involves the person who is essential in the film industry to manage the finances and financial records during the film production. Working in this position requires being in close association with the producer and the production office for the development of the film budget and to arrange schedules. Further into this role, as the accountant for a film, day-to-day duties are expected such as the normal accounting tasks of an office and maintaining the budget by recording the expenses accumulated to make secure they do not go over the allocated budget.

Other duties of the production accountant include:

- Managing the payroll
- Managing the petty cash
- Analysing costs
- Provide weekly cash reports
- Estimating future costs

Throughput Accounting

Throughput Accounting (TA) can be understood as a simplified accounting system based on Theory of Constraints (ToC) principles. TA makes growth-driven management and decision making simpler and understandable even for people not familiar with traditional accounting.

Beyond simplifying, TA has a different approach compared to traditional accounting. The latter will focus on cost control (cost of goods sold) and minimizing the unit cost-while TA strives to maximize profit.

Throughput Accounting sets the base for Throughput Analysis, helping to make decisions in the ToC way.

Simplifying Accounting

Throughput Accounting will probably not replace GAAP in short nor medium term, but provides a limited set of simple KPIs, sufficient to:

- Manage and make decisions in a growth-oriented and ToC way.
- Allow faster reporting and near to real-time figure-based management.
- Help people in operations to understand the basics of accounting.
- Set a common base for controllers and operations to discuss decisions, investments, etc.

Throughput Accounting uses 3 KPIs and 2 ratios:

Throughput (T)

Throughput, defined as the rate of producing goal units (usually money) and translates as revenue or sales minus totally variable expenses in accounting terms.

Totally variable expenses can be simplified to the cost of direct materials because labor is nowadays paid on a (relatively) fixed amount per time period, hence a constant expense to be considered as part of Operating Expenses.

Operating Expenses (OE)

Operating Expenses are all expenses, except the totally variable expenses previously mentioned in the calculation of throughput, required to run and maintain the system of production. Operating Expenses are considered fixed costs, even so they may have some variable cost characteristics.

Investments (I)

Investments, formerly call Inventories, is the amount of cash invested (formerly "tied") into the system in order to turn as much of the Investments into Throughput as possible. This encompasses the stored raw material waiting to be transformed into sellable products as well as investments in capacities/capabilities to produce more units.

Net Profit (NP)

Net Profit is defined as Throughput minus Operating Expenses, or Sales – Total Variable Costs – Operating Expenses.

Return on Investment (ROI)

Return On Investment is the Net Profit compared to Investments:

(ROI = NP/I).

Drivers for Achieving the Goal

Throughput Accounting offers a simplified way to identify and use the drivers to achieve the Goal, assuming the Goal is to make money now and in the future.

In a very simple way this can be summarized by the following picture which means strive to maximize Throughput while minimize the Operating Expenses and Investments.

ToC practitioners recognize that Throughput has no limit while Operating Expenses and Investments have limits beyond which no safe operations can be further envisioned.

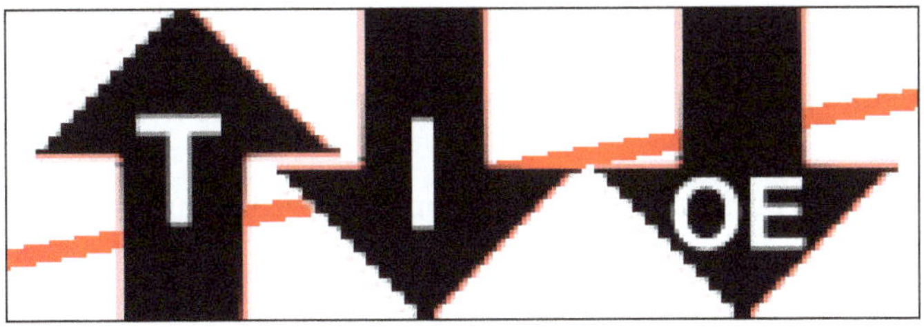

The priority focus on improving T (focusing on the constraint exploitation) rather to go for all-out cost cutting explains the (usually) superior results when going the ToC way compared to unfocused improvements.

Throughput Accounting KPIs can be presented in a Dupont-inspired model in order to make the levers and consequences clear.

Throughput Analysis

Beyond the simplification compared to traditional accounting, Throughput Accounting sets the base for Throughput Analysis, helping to make decisions in the ToC way.

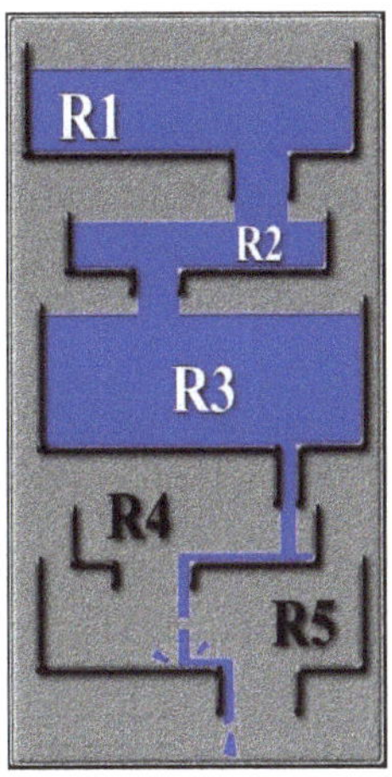

Reminder: In a system with a capacity constraint, the Throughput is limited and controlled by the sole constraint. As the capacity is fully used and no spare is available to exploit, what goes through the constraint must be chosen wisely in order to make the best use of this very precious resource.

It becomes obvious then that utmost attention must be paid to maximize the passing of the highest profit generating products through the constraint. The decision making is then based on the Throughput per constraint minute rate. The higher the T/mn, the better.

Other decisions: Throughput Analysis helps to make are about anything likely to alter the Throughput, Operating Expenses or investments. Basically, any incremental increase of OE and/or I should lead to an incremental increase of T.

References

- What-are-the-different-types-of-cost-accounting, accounting: backoffice.com.sg, Retrieved 28 February, 2019
- Methods-of-Costing, business: toughnickel.com, Retrieved 4 August, 2019
- Costing-methods: edupristine.com, Retrieved 9 April, 2019
- Activity-based-costing-method: lumenlearning.com, Retrieved 11 July, 2019
- Activity-based-costing: accountingcoach.com, Retrieved 13 January, 2019
- Advantages-and-demerits-of-activity-based-costing-abc, costing, accounting: yourarticlelibrary.com, Retrieved 23 February, 2019
- Kaplan, Robert S. and Bruns, W. Accounting and Management: A Field Study Perspective (Harvard Business School Press, 1987) ISBN 0-87584-186-4
- Advantages-and-disadvantages-of-standard-costing, cost-accounting: businesswritingservices.org, Retrieved 19 June, 2019
- Monden, Yasuhiro & Kazuki Hamada (1991). "Target costing and kaizen costing in Japanese automobile companies". Journal of Management Accounting Research
- Marginal-costing: businessjargons.com, Retrieved 7 March, 2019
- Advantages-and-Disadvantages-of-Marginal-Costing, business: toughnickel.com, Retrieved 11 March, 2019
- Definition-lean-accounting: bizfluent.com, Retrieved 21 January, 2019
- What-is-throughput-accounting: hohmannchris.wordpress.com, Retrieved 10 May, 2019

6

Managing Cost

There are a number of different tools which are used for managing cost such as capital budgeting, cost variability, capacity management and inventory valuation. The chapter closely examines these key methods of managing cost as well as details the different types of capital budgeting to provide an extensive understanding of the subject.

Capital Budgeting

Capital budgeting is a company's formal process used for evaluating potential expenditures or investments that are significant in amount. It involves the decision to invest the current funds for addition, disposition, modification or replacement of fixed assets. The large expenditures include the purchase of fixed assets like land and building, new equipments, rebuilding or replacing existing equipments, research and development, etc. The large amounts spent for these types of projects are known as capital expenditures. Capital Budgeting is a tool for maximizing a company's future profits since most companies are able to manage only a limited number of large projects at any one time.

Capital budgeting usually involves calculation of each project's future accounting profit by period, the cash flow by period, the present value of cash flows after considering time value of money, the number of years it takes for a project's cash flow to pay back the initial cash investment, an assessment of risk, and various other factors.

Capital is the total investment of the company and budgeting is the art of building budgets.

Features of Capital Budgeting

1. It involves high risk.
2. Large profits are estimated.
3. Long time period between the initial investments and estimated returns.

Capital Budgeting Process

Project Identification and Generation

The first step towards capital budgeting is to generate a proposal for investments. There could be various reasons for taking up investments in a business. It could be addition of a new product line or expanding the existing one. It could be a proposal to either increase the production or reduce the costs of outputs.

Project Screening and Evaluation

This step mainly involves selecting all correct criteria's to judge the desirability of a proposal. This has to match the objective of the firm to maximize its market value. The tool of time value of money comes handy in this step.

Also the estimation of the benefits and the costs needs to be done. The total cash inflow and outflow along with the uncertainties and risks associated with the proposal has to be analyzed thoroughly and appropriate provisioning has to be done for the same.

Project Selection

There is no such defined method for the selection of a proposal for investments as different businesses have different requirements. That is why, the approval of an investment proposal is done based on the selection criteria and screening process which is defined for every firm keeping in mind the objectives of the investment being undertaken.

Once the proposal has been finalized, the different alternatives for raising or acquiring funds have to be explored by the finance team. This is called preparing the capital budget. The average cost of funds has to be reduced. A detailed procedure for periodical reports and tracking the project for the lifetime needs to be streamlined in the initial phase itself. The final approvals are based on profitability, Economic constituents, viability and market conditions.

Implementation

Money is spent and thus proposal is implemented. The different responsibilities like implementing the proposals, completion of the project within the requisite time period and reduction of cost are allotted. The management then takes up the task of monitoring and containing the implementation of the proposals.

Performance Review

The final stage of capital budgeting involves comparison of actual results with the standard ones. The unfavorable results are identified and removing the various difficulties of the projects helps for future selection and execution of the proposals.

Table: Factors Affecting Capital Budgeting.

Availability of Funds	Working Capital
Structure of Capital	Capital Return
Management decisions	Need of the project
Accounting methods	Government policy

Taxation policy	Earnings
Lending terms of financial institutions	Economic value of the project

Capital Budgeting Decisions

The crux of capital budgeting is profit maximization. There are two ways to it; either increase the revenues or reduce the costs. The increase in revenues can be achieved by expansion of operations by adding a new product line. Reducing costs means representing obsolete return on assets.

- Accept/Reject decision: If a proposal is accepted, the firm invests in it and if rejected the firm does not invest. Generally, proposals that yield a rate of return greater than a certain required rate of return or cost of capital are accepted and the others are rejected. All independent projects are accepted. Independent projects are projects that do not compete with one another in such a way that acceptance gives a fair possibility of acceptance of another.
- Mutually exclusive project decision: Mutually exclusive projects compete with other projects in such a way that the acceptance of one will exclude the acceptance of the other projects. Only one may be chosen. Mutually exclusive investment decisions gain importance when more than one proposal is acceptable under the accept/reject decision. The acceptance of the best alternative eliminates the other alternatives.
- Capital rationing decision: In a situation where the firm has unlimited funds, capital budgeting becomes a very simple process. In that, independent investment proposals yielding a return greater than some predetermined level are accepted. But actual business has a different picture. They have fixed capital budget with large number of investment proposals competing for it. Capital rationing refers to the situation where the firm has more acceptable investments requiring a greater amount of finance than that is available with the firm. Ranking of the investment project is employed on the basis of some predetermined criterion such as the rate of return. The project with highest return is ranked first and the acceptable projects are ranked thereafter.

Capital Budgeting Methods

There are a number of methods commonly used to evaluate fixed assets under a formal capital budgeting system. The more important ones are:

- Net present value analysis: Identify the net change in cash flows associated with a fixed asset purchase, and discount them to their present value. Then compare all proposed projects with positive net present values, and accept those with the highest net present values until funds run out.

- Constraint analysis: Identify the bottleneck machine or work center in a production environment and invest in those fixed assets that maximize the utilization of the bottleneck operation. Under this approach, you are less likely to invest in areas downstream from the bottleneck operation (since they are constrained by the bottleneck operation) and more likely to invest upstream from the bottleneck (since additional capacity there makes it easier to keep the bottleneck fully supplied with inventory).
- Payback period: Determine the period required to generate sufficient cash flow from a project to pay for the initial investment in it. This is essentially a risk measure, for the focus is on the period of time that the investment is at risk of not being returned to the company.
- Avoidance analysis: Determine whether increased maintenance can be used to prolong the life of existing assets, rather than investing in replacement assets. This analysis can substantially reduce a company's total investment in fixed assets.

The Importance of Capital Budgeting

The amount of cash involved in a fixed asset investment may be so large that it could lead to the bankruptcy of a firm if the investment fails. Consequently, capital budgeting is a mandatory activity for larger fixed asset proposals. This is less of an issue for smaller investments; in these latter cases, it is better to streamline the capital budgeting process substantially, so that the focus is more on getting the investments made as expeditiously as possible; by doing so, the operations of profit centers are not hindered by the analysis of their fixed asset proposals.

Types of Capital Budgeting

Throughput Analysis

Throughput analysis is the most complicated form of capital budgeting analysis but also the most accurate in helping managers decide which projects to pursue. Under this method, the entire company is considered as a single profit-generating system. Throughput is measured as an amount of material passing through that system.

The analysis assumes that nearly all costs are operating expenses, that a company needs to maximize the throughput of the entire system to pay for expenses, and that the way to maximize profits is to maximize the throughput passing through a bottleneck operation. A bottleneck is the resource in the system that requires the longest time in operations.

This means that managers should always place a higher priority on capital budgeting projects that will increase throughput passing through the bottleneck.

DCF Analysis

Discounted cash flow (DCF) analysis looks at the initial cash outflow needed to fund a project, the mix of cash inflows in the form of revenue, and other future outflows in the form of maintenance and other costs.

These costs, except for the initial outflow, are discounted back to the present date. The resulting number from the DCF analysis is the net present value (NPV). Projects with the highest NPV should rank over others unless one or more are mutually exclusive.

Payback Analysis

Payback analysis is the simplest form of capital budgeting analysis but it's also the least accurate. It's still widely used because it's quick and can give managers a "back of the envelope" understanding of the real value of a proposed project.

This analysis calculates how long it will take to recoup the costs of an investment. The payback period is identified by dividing the initial investment in the project by the average yearly cash inflow that the project will generate.

Cost Variability

Cost is an essential aspect of running a business. It is the expenditure that is incurred to run any business. Every resource used in production has an associated cost attached to it. Be it labor, raw material, assets, human resources, administration etc.; all bear some cost. Businesses keep a track of the costs of the companies and analyze them from time to time so as to find the best alternatives and minimize the cost.

Understanding costs need relating it to the various processes of business i.e. production, selling or holding up assets. Some costs can be directly related to the quantity of production or output or the level of selling. For example, the cost of raw material is directly attributable to the quantity of production whereas the selling cost is associated with the number of units sold.

Variability refers to the frequent variations of fluctuations in the data. It is the extent to which the data diverge from the average of the data. Thus, cost variability refers to the changes in the cost of the company. Upon the basis of the variability, the costs can be categorized into the following three:

Fixed Cost

Fixed cost refers to the cost that does not change at all in the given period of time irrespective of the change in the production. The fixed cost remains constant even if the production falls to zero. Fixed Cost as defined by ICMA (U.K.), "A cost which tends to be unaffected by variations in the volume of output. Fixed Costs depend mainly on the effluxion of time and do not vary with volume or rate of output." The fixed costs are more famously known as standby costs, period costs or capacity cost. The fixed cost remains constant only in short period of time. In the longer run, it tends to become a variable cost as changes can be made to it as per the requirement and capacity.

The fixed costs are the necessary payments to be made by the business for running it. The major aim of any fresh business is to cover its fixed costs. When it covers its fixed costs, it is said to be on a break-even point. If the business fails in achieving that it will have to shut down its business. These fixed costs are not purely for the manufacturing process. These can be other payments as well such as rent, taxes, salary etc. They have to be paid after every decided interval and cannot be foregone. These salaries can be changed over a period of time but they are not variable. They remain fixed.

The fixed costs in total are constant but when attributed to a fixed cost per unit; it tends to fall with the increase in the number of the units produced. The fixed cost can be understood using the following example:

A company incurs a monthly rent of $5,000 per month. This will be borne by the company even if it does on operate. In return, the company will charge this cost from its customer. If the company produces 1,000 units, $5 (5000/ 1000) will be allocated to each product i.e. fixes cost per unit. If it increases the scale of production to 2,000 units, the fixed cost per unit will fall down to $2.5 (5000/ 2000).

This can be illustrated by the following graph:

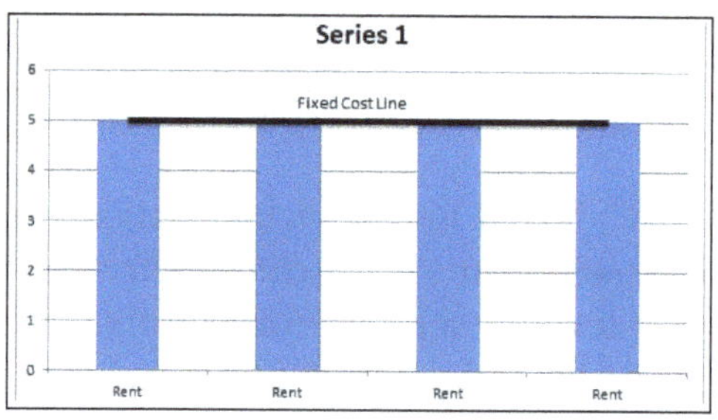

When the fixed cost will be studied with the production units, the fixed cost per unit will come out to be as follows:

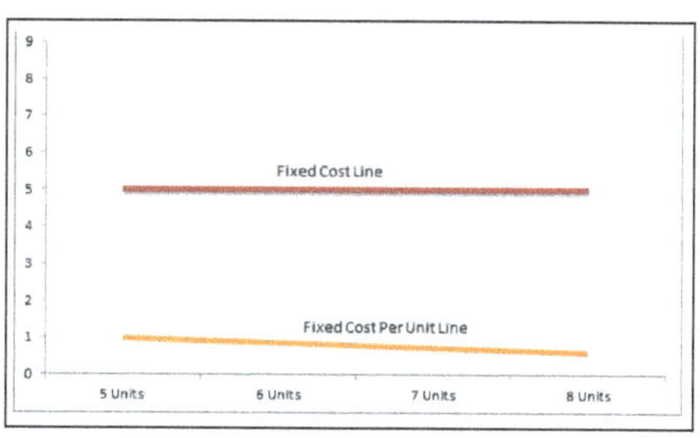

The fixed costs can be further categorized into following:

1. Committed Costs: Committed costs are the costs that the business or the managers are under obligation to pay or have committed to pay. These costs are important for the establishment and physical existence of the business. Such commitment costs never change for a given period of time. These cannot be readily changed. These cannot be eliminated and stays with the company. Examples for such committed costs are Depreciation, Taxes, Insurance and Rent etc. These are to be paid by the business anyhow. In case the business fails to pay such costs, the business will be facing a shut- down situation.

2. Managed Costs: Managed costs are the costs that have to be incurred for running the current operation in the company for e.g. Manufacturing, transportation etc. These are generally the salaries or wages to be paid.

3. Discretionary Costs: Sometimes there are certain decisions or policies that are made by the company or the managers which require funds or costs to be incurred. These are at the discretion of the managers and can be readily altered as per their convenience.

4. Step- Costs: The step costs are partly variable and partly fixed. But these are different from the fixed These costs remain variable for a given amount of output and fixed for a given amount of output. These form a graph just like steps of a stair. This can be seen as follows:

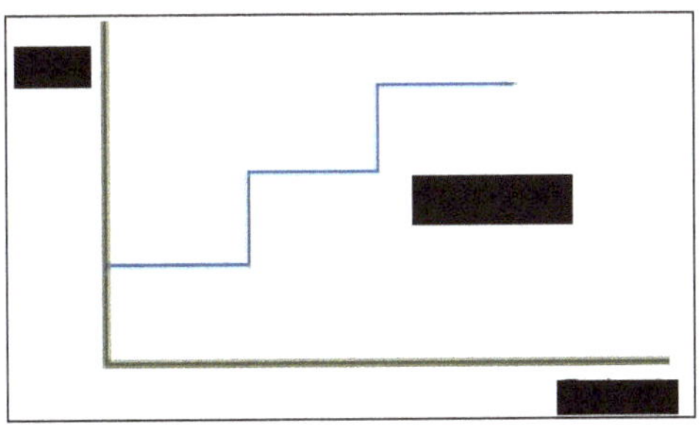

Variable Cost

Variable Cost refers to the cost that varies in proportion to the units produced. The variable cost in totality increases with the increase in the number of units produced. This means the variable cost is directly proportional to the number of units produced. However, it is to be noted that the variable cost increases in totality with the increase in the number of units. The variable cost per unit remains the same or constant. The variable cost includes:

1. Direct Material Cost,
2. Direct Labor Cost, and
3. Direct Expenses

All these together contribute to the variable cost. So, if the cost of producing a single unit involves employing 1 unit of raw material, 1 hour of labor and $1 as direct expenses; provided further that the cost of raw material is $5 per unit and the wages for 1 hour labor is $5, the total variable cost of the product will be $5 + $5 + $1 = $11. Thus, with every unit produced, the total variable cost will be increased by $11. This can be illustrated by the following graph:

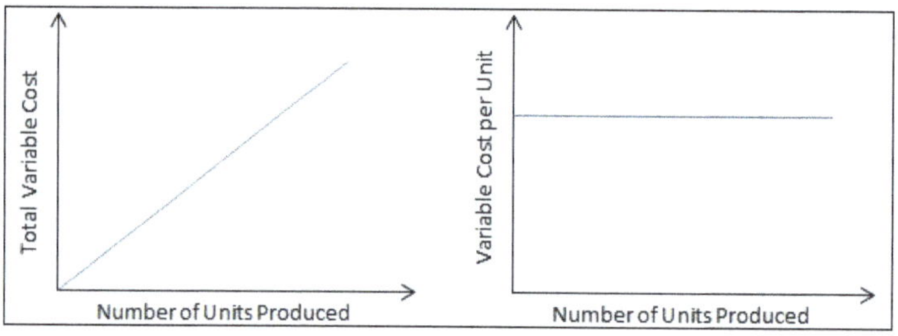

Mixed Cost

Mixed cost refers to a mix of both fixed as well as variable cost. It is a combination of the variable as well as a fixed cost which is why it is known as Semi-variable cost. As per the traits of both variable and fixed costs, they tend to increase with the increase in the production but at the same time they tend to remain constant and do not change with the change in the production. In simpler words, it tends to remain constant or fixed up to a certain level; and once it is crossed, they tend to become variable. This type of costs can be seen in the business areas where the workers are paid on the basis of the units produced by them along with a fixed pay. In case the business's capacity increases, that also amounts to an increase in the variable cost but keeping the fixed cost constant.

This can be understood using the following example:

A company is paying its employees an amount of $1000 as fixed salary for any number of units he produces. If he exceeds the production level i.e. 100 units, he will get paid $12 for every extra unit he produces.

Now, the graph for such a salary will remain till the employee produces 100 units. Once he exceeds the 100th unit, the graph will turn into a variable one where it will increase by $12 for every unit he produces. Such a graph will be drawn:

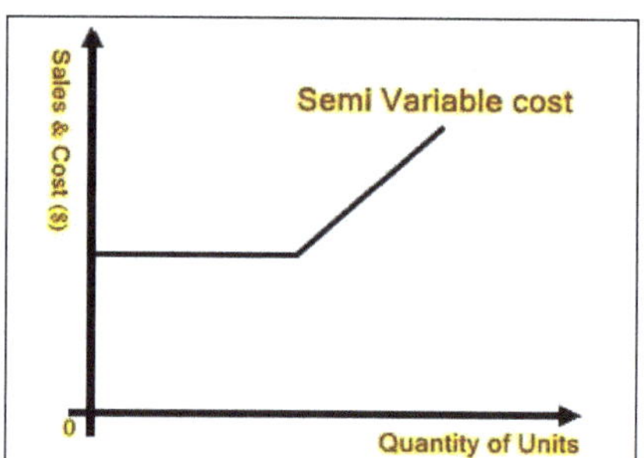

Semi-Variable cost Chart

Mathematically, the mixed cost can be represented as follows:

Mixed Cost = Total Fixed Cost + (Units * Variable Cost per unit)

Cost Variance

Cost variance is the difference between the actual amount of a cost and its budgeted or planned amount. For example, if a company had actual repairs expense of $950 for May but the budgeted amount was $800, the company had a cost variance of $150. When the actual cost is more than the budgeted amount, the cost variance is said to be unfavorable. When an actual cost is less than the budgeted amount, the cost variance is said to be favorable.

Cost Variances in Standard Costing Systems

Cost variances are a key part of the standard costing system used by some manufacturers. In such a system, the cost variances direct attention to the difference between 1) the standard, predetermined and expected costs of the good output, and 2) the actual manufacturing costs incurred. These cost variances send a signal to management that the company is experiencing actual costs that are different from the company's plan.

Standard costing systems report a minimum of two cost variances for each of the following manufacturing costs:

- Direct materials
- Direct labor
- Manufacturing overhead

Manufacturing Overhead

Manufacturing overhead (also known as factory overhead, factory burden, production overhead) involves a company's manufacturing operations. It includes the costs incurred in the manufacturing facilities *other than the costs of direct materials and direct labor*. Hence, manufacturing overhead is referred to as an *indirect cost*.

Generally accepted accounting principles require that a manufacturer's inventory and the cost of goods sold shall consist of:

- The cost of direct materials,
- The cost of direct labor,
- The cost of manufacturing overhead.

Expenses that are outside of the manufacturing facilities, such as selling, general and administrative expenses, are not product costs and are *not* inventoriable. They are reported as expenses on the income statement in the accounting period in which they occur.

Examples of Manufacturing Overhead

Some examples of manufacturing overhead costs include the following:

- Depreciation, rent and property taxes on the manufacturing facilities.
- Depreciation on the manufacturing equipment.
- Managers and supervisors in the manufacturing facilities.
- Repairs and maintenance employees in the manufacturing facilities.
- Electricity and gas used in the manufacturing facilities.
- Indirect factory supplies, and much more.

Because manufacturing overhead is an indirect cost, accountants are faced with the task of *assigning* or *allocating* overhead costs to each of the units produced. This is a challenging task because there may be no direct relationship. For example, the property taxes and insurance on the manufacturing buildings are based on the assets' value and not on the number of units manufactured. Yet these and other indirect costs must be allocated to the units manufactured.

Cost of Quality

Cost of Quality is a methodology used to define and measure where and what amount of an organization's resources are being used for prevention activities and maintaining product quality as opposed to the costs resulting from internal and external failures. The Cost of Quality can be represented by the sum of two factors. The Cost of Good Quality and the Cost of Poor Quality equals the Cost of Quality, as represented in the basic equation below:

CoQ = CoGQ + CoPQ

The Cost of Quality equation looks simple but in reality it is more complex. The Cost of Quality includes all costs associated with the quality of a product from preventive costs intended to reduce or eliminate failures, cost of process controls to maintain quality levels and the costs related to failures both internal and external.

Implementation of Cost of Quality (COQ)

Effective use and implementation of Cost of Quality methodology enables an organization to accurately measure the amount of resources being used for Cost of Good

Quality and Cost of Poor Quality. With this valuable information the organization can determine where to allocate resources to improve product quality and the bottom line. To further illustrate the value of cost of quality, review the following example. The name of the company has been changed but the content represents actual events and results.

Alpha Company once measured Cost of Quality as the amount of warranty cost versus total sales. This method only examined the Cost of Poor Quality. This data did reveal a problem area in the facility. It was discovered that customer part shortages originating from one work cell were resulting in warranty costs of over $400,000 in one year. A team was formed to investigate and perform Root Cause Analysis (RCA) of the shortages and a plan was developed to redesign the work cell for an estimated cost of $60,000. With management approval, the work cell was redesigned with a revised layout, pick bins, dedicated locations for all the parts, process controls were defined and implemented and several additional improvements were made. The changes reduced tact times and the number of operators required for the process. This provided resources for the addition of quality technicians to regularly audit and maintain the process on all shifts. Within the first year of operation, shortages were reduced by 50% equaling a $200,000 reduction in warranty costs. The project resulted in a positive impact on the bottom line of $140,000 in the first year. Alpha Company has since implemented processes to measure and reduce scrap, improved process controls and introduced new quality metrics throughout the organization. They are now actively measuring and evaluating both the cost of good quality and poor quality.

In the example above, the Cost of Poor Quality (CoPQ) was having a major impact on the bottom line. Through an investment in the Cost of Good Quality (CoGQ), Alpha Company achieved a significant reduction in the Cost of Quality. There are opportunities for improvement in processes at most organizations. It has been estimated that the Cost of Quality usually amounts to between 15-40% of business costs. The goal of implementing Cost of Quality methodology is to maximize product quality while minimizing cost. Cost of Quality methodology provides the detailed information that management needs to accurately evaluate the effectiveness of their quality systems, identify problem areas and opportunities for improvement.

Measurement of COQ

The methods for calculating Cost of Quality vary from company to company. In many cases, organizations like the one described in the previous example, determine the Cost of Quality by calculating total warranty dollars as a percentage of sales. Unfortunately this method is only looking externally at the Cost of Quality and not looking internally. In order to gain a better understanding, a more comprehensive look at all quality costs is required.

The Cost of Quality can be divided into four categories. They include Prevention, Appraisal, Internal Failure and External Failure. Within each of the four categories there are numerous possible sources of cost related to good or poor quality. Some examples of typical sources of Cost of Quality are listed.

Cost of Good Quality (CoGQ)

- Prevention Costs – Costs incurred from activities intended to keep failures to a minimum. These can include, but are not limited to, the following:
    - Establishing Product Specifications,
    - Quality Planning,
    - New Product Development and Testing,
    - Development of a Quality Management System (QMS),
    - Proper Employee Training.
- Appraisal Costs – Costs incurred to maintain acceptable product quality levels. Appraisal costs can include, but are not limited to, the following:
    - Incoming Material Inspections,
    - Process Controls,
    - Check Fixtures,
    - Quality Audits,
    - Supplier Assessments.

Cost of Poor Quality (CoPQ)

- Internal Failures – Costs associated with defects found before the product or service reaches the customer. Internal Failures may include, but are not limited to, the following examples:
    - Excessive Scrap,
    - Product Re-work,
    - Waste due to poorly designed processes,
    - Machine breakdown due to improper maintenance,
    - Costs associated with failure analysis.
- External Failures – Costs associated with defects found after the customer receives the product or service. External Failures may include, but are not limited to, the following examples:
    - Service and Repair Costs,

- Warranty Claims,
- Customer Complaints,
- Product or Material Returns,
- Incorrect Sales Orders,
- Incomplete BOMs,
- Shipping Damage due to Inadequate Packaging.

These four categories can now be applied to the original Cost of Quality equation. Our original equation stated that the Cost of Quality is the sum of Cost of Good Quality and Cost of Poor Quality. This is still true however the basic equation can be expanded by applying the categories within both the Cost of Good Quality and the Cost of Poor Quality.

- The Cost of Good Quality is the sum of Prevention Cost and Appraisal Cost (CoGQ = PC + AC)
- The Cost of Poor Quality is the sum of Internal and External Failure Costs (CoPQ = IFC + EFC)

By combining the equations, Cost of Quality can be more accurately defined, as shown in the equation below:

$$COQ = (PC + AC) + (IFC + EFC)$$

One important factor to note is that the Cost of Quality equation is non-linear. Investing in the Cost of Good Quality does not necessarily mean that the overall Cost of Quality will increase. In fact, when the resources are invested in the right areas, the Cost of Quality should decrease. When failures are prevented/detected prior to leaving the facility and reaching the customer, Cost of Poor Quality will be reduced.

Cost of Equity

In finance, the cost of equity is the return (often expressed as a rate of return) a firm theoretically pays to its equity investors, i.e., shareholders, to compensate for the risk they undertake by investing their capital. Firms need to acquire capital from others to operate and grow. Individuals and organizations who are willing to provide their funds to others naturally desire to be rewarded. Just as landlords seek rents on their property, capital providers seek returns on their funds, which must be commensurate with the risk undertaken.

Firms obtain capital from two kinds of sources: lenders and equity investors. From the perspective of capital providers, lenders seek to be rewarded with interest and equity investors seek dividends and/or appreciation in the value of their investment (capital gain). From a firm's perspective, they must pay for the capital it obtains from others, which is called its cost of capital. Such costs are separated into a firm's cost of debt and cost of equity and attributed to these two kinds of capital sources.

While a firm's present cost of debt is relatively easy to determine from observation of interest rates in the capital markets, its current cost of equity is unobservable and must be estimated. Finance theory and practice offers various models for estimating a particular firm's cost of equity such as the capital asset pricing model, or CAPM. Another method is derived from the Gordon Model, which is a discounted cash flow model based on dividend returns and eventual capital return from the sale of the investment. Another simple method is the Bond Yield Plus Risk Premium (BYPRP), where a subjective risk premium is added to the firm's long-term debt interest rate. In addition, the cost of equity can be calculated by using the discounted residual income model to estimate the market implied cost-of-capital. The paper shows that a firm's implied cost-of-capital is a function of its industry membership, B/M ratio, forecasted long-term growth rate, and the dispersion in analyst earnings forecasts. Moreover, a firm's overall cost of capital, which consists of the two types of capital costs, can be estimated using the weighted average cost of capital model.

According to finance theory, as a firm's risk increases/decreases, its cost of capital increases/decreases. This theory is linked to observation of human behavior and logic: capital providers expect reward for offering their funds to others. Such providers are usually rational and prudent preferring safety over risk. They naturally require an extra reward as an incentive to place their capital in a riskier investment instead of a safer one. If an investment's risk increases, capital providers demand higher returns or they will place their capital elsewhere.

Knowing a firm's cost of capital is needed in order to make better decisions. Managers make capital budgeting decisions while capital providers make decisions about lending and investment. Such decisions can be made after quantitative analysis that typically uses a firm's cost of capital as a model input.

Cost of Capital

Cost of capital is the opportunity cost of funds available to a company for investment in different projects. The most common measure of cost of capital is the weighted average cost of capital, which is a composite measure of marginal return required on all components of the company's capital, namely debt, preferred stock and common stock.

Most companies are for-profit entities which must generate wealth for its shareholders and debt-holders. The projects they invest in must earn enough to pay off the interest on bonds and other debt and pay cash dividends to shareholders and/or generate enough growth to cause an increase in their stock price. It is important for companies to calculate the cost of different components of capital, identify their target mix of debt and equity and work out their weighted average cost of capital. In deciding whether to invest in a project or not, through the capital budgeting process, they must compare the return available on the project with the cost of capital and accept the project only where the return is higher than the cost of capital. If they invest in projects with return lower than the cost of capital, they are effectively destroying their shareholders wealth.

Formula: Weighted average cost of capital is calculated by multiplying the after-tax cost of debt with the percentage of debt in total capital, multiplying the cost of preferred stock with the percentage of preferred stock in total capital, multiplying the cost of common stock with the percentage of common stock in total capital and summing all the products together.

The following equation mathematically expresses the definition of WACC:

$$\text{Cost of Capital} = w_d \times r_d \times (1-t) + w_p + w_e \times r_e$$

Where wd, wp and we refer to the relative percentage of debt, preferred stock and common stock in the total target capital. r_d, r_p and r_e are cost of debt, cost of preferred stock and cost of common stock respectively. r_d is multiplied by (1 – t), where *t* refers to the tax rate, because interest expense is allowed as deduction while calculating taxes and this tax-deductibility creates a saving which must be accounted for.

WACC Calculator:

Capital	Common	Preferred	Debt
Weight ($ or %):	68.5	0	31.5
Cost %:	10.88	0	4.50
Tax Rate %:			30
WACC %:	8.45		

Component Cost of Capital

If a company's debt is publicly traded and market prices are available, cost of debt can be determined as equal to its yield to maturity. If no reasonable estimate of market price is available but a bond rating is available, a company's cost of debt can be estimated as equal to the average cost of debt of companies in the same industry which have the same bond rating. If no market price or bond rating is available for the company's debt, a rating might be estimated based on financial ratios.

Cost of preferred stock can be calculated using the following formula:

$$\text{Cost of Preferred Stock} = \frac{\text{Preferred Divideds Per Share}}{\text{Current Preffered Stock Price}}$$

Cost of common stock can be estimated using either the capital asset pricing model. Under the capital asset pricing mode, cost of common equity is calculated as follows:

$$\text{Cost of Common Stock} = r_f + \text{beta} \times \text{MRP}$$

Where r_f stands for risk-free rate, typically estimated as equivalent to 10-year government bond rate. Beta is the beta coefficient of the company, a measure which assesses the sensitivity of the company's common stock to movement in market interest rates.

MRP stands for market risk premium (also called equity risk premium) which equals the expected return on the broad market index such as S & P 500 i.e E_m minus the risk-free rate i.e. r_f.

$$\text{Market Risk Premium(MRP)} = E_m - r_f$$

If no reliable estimate of MRP is available, the historical risk premium approach maybe used, which bases market risk premium on the historical average of market risk premium.

Under the dividend discount model, cost of common stock can be estimated as follows:

$$\text{Cost of Common Stock} = \frac{D_1}{P_0} + g$$

Where D_1 is the dividend per share expected in 1 year and P_0 is the current market price of the stock and g is the sustainable growth rate.

Relative Weights

The weighted average cost of capital weighs different component cost of capital in proportion of their relative weight in the target capital structure.

The proportions must be calculated based on market values instead of book values and they should be based on target capital structure, the capital mix the company wants to ultimately achieve, even if it differs materially from its current capital structure.

Example:

Let's calculate weighted average cost of capital of The Walt Disney Company.

The following information is available from Morningstar for the FY 2017:

Dividend per share	$1.56
5-year average return on equity	18.47%
Dividend payout ratio	27.6%
Debt to equity ratio	0.46
Current stock price	$109.20

From Yahoo Finance, we find that the company's beta coefficient is 1.37, from NYU Stern website's historical implied risk premiums, we find that the latest is 5.9% (as compared to the historical geometric average of 4.8%). The latest US 10-year treasury bond yield is 2.8%. Assume that the weighted average effective interest rate on the company's borrowings is 4.5% and its tax rate is 30%.

First, we need to find the component cost of capital. The cost of debt is 4.5% because it is the effective interest rate on debt. The company has no preferred stock. The cost of common stock can be calculated using three approaches:

- The capital asset pricing model,
- The dividend discount model and
- The historical equity risk premium approach.

Under the capital asset pricing model, cost of common stock equals 10.88%:

$$\begin{aligned}\text{Cost of Common Stock}(\text{CAPM}) &= 2.8\% + 1.37 \times 5.9\% \\ &= 10.88\%\end{aligned}$$

To calculate the cost of equity using the dividend discount model, we need to work out the sustainable growth rate, which equals the product of return on equity and retention rate (which in turn equals 1 minus the dividend payout ratio).

$$\begin{aligned}\text{Growth Rate}(g) &= (1 - \text{Dividend Payout Ratio}) \times \text{ROE} \\ &= (1 - 27.6\%) \times 18.47\% \\ &= 13.37\%\end{aligned}$$

Under the dividend discount model, cost of common stock works out to 14.99%:

$$\begin{aligned}\text{Cost of Common Stock}(\text{DDM}) &= \frac{\$1.56 \times (1 + 13.37\%)}{\$109.20} + 13.37\% \\ &= 14.99\%\end{aligned}$$

Under the historical equity risk premium approach, DIS cost of common stock is 9.38%:

$$\text{Cost of Common Stock}\,(\text{HRPA}) = 2.8\% + 1.37 \times 4.8\%$$
$$= 9.38\%$$

Since DIS is a well-established large-cap company, using the CAPM cost of equity estimate is appropriate.

We need to find their relative proportions which we can work out from the debt to equity ratio.

Debt/Equity = 0.46

Debt/(Assets – Debt) = 0.46

Debt = 0.46 × (Assets – Debt)

Debt + 0.46 × Debt = 0.46 × Assets

$$\frac{\text{Debt}}{\text{Assets}} = \frac{0.46}{1.46} = 31.5\%$$

$$\frac{\text{Equity}}{\text{Assets}} = 1 - \frac{\text{Debt}}{\text{Assets}} = 1 - 31.5\% = 68.5\%$$

Now that we have all the necessary figures, we just need to plug the relevant numbers in the WACC formula:

$$\text{WACC} = 31.5\% \times 4.5\% \times (1 - 30\%) + 68.5\% \times 10.88\% = 8.45\%$$

Capacity Management

Levels of Activity

The following four major levels of activity used in capacity management:

Normal Activity

This can be defined as the rate of activity needed to meet average sales demand over a period that is sufficiently long to cover seasonal, cyclical and trend variations in the pattern of demand for company's products.

Such a rate of activity will be influenced very largely by market factors in conjunction with the physical limits of plant capacity. If sales do not vary much from year to year, this will be equivalent to expected activity. A rule of thumb is to take normal activity to represent 75% to 90% of practical capacity.

Expected Activity

The expected activity is the rate of activity that is expected to prevail over the next year. This method is considered to be more appropriate than normal activity when environmental conditions prevent reliable forecasts being made for periods in excess of one year.

Practical Capacity

This measure represents the maximum level at which a company can realistically operate at full efficiency. This allows for unavoidable operating interruptions such as the need for maintenance work to be carried out and waiting time which means that practical capacity is less than ideal capacity. Nevertheless, the concept of practical capacity is an introspective engineering concept that pays no attention to current or expected demand conditions.

The effectiveness of the measure depends on stability of demand giving stability of operations. In other words, given a ready market for its output and no distribution problems, practical capacity is that level of activity at which most managements would wish to operate.

Ideal Capacity

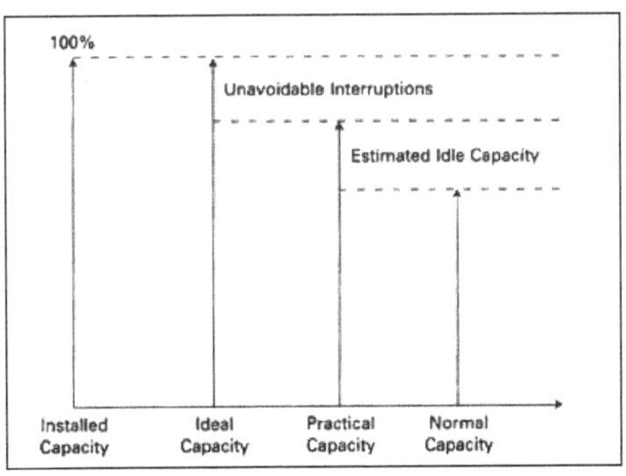

Levels of production capacity.

This is the maximum number of operating hours that could be available ignoring the stoppages due to down time, repairs etc. No attention is paid to demand conditions which emphasizes the artificial nature of the measure. It represents a theoretical ideal that can be used as a bench mark. For example, practical capacity is usually taken to be 75% to 85% of ideal capacity.

The relationship amongst these concepts of capacity is shown in figure in which normal activity is taken to include expected activity for simplicity.

Between the 100% maximum of ideal capacity and the more realistic practical capacity there is a gap due to inevitable but acceptable interruptions, considered from the view point of the industrial engineer. A further gap exists between practical capacity and normal capacity which allows for the contingencies of uncertainty and environmental fluctuations.

Idle Capacity Costs

Idle capacity is that part of capacity of a plant, machinery or equipment which cannot be effectively utilised in production, due to lack of demand, shortage of raw material, power, labour etc. Idle capacity is the difference between the practical capacity and capacity utilised.

The idle capacity may exist due to internal problems or problems beyond the control of organisation. The costs associated with the idle capacity are generally of fixed in nature like depreciation, repairs and maintenance, insurance premium, rent, management and supervisory costs. These costs cannot be absorbed fully due to under utilisation of capacity available with the organisation.

$$\text{Idle capacity cost} = \frac{\text{Total Overhead of Plant}}{\text{Practical Capacity}} \times \text{Idle capacity}$$

The idle capacity costs are treated in the cost accounts in the following ways:

1. Idle capacity costs due to unavoidable causes are absorbed into capacity utilised.
2. Idle capacity costs due to avoidable causes are transferred to Costing profit and loss account.
3. Idle capacity costs due to seasonal fluctuations are absorbed into the cost of production by using supplementary overhead rates.

Cost Control

Cost control is a tool of management executives to regulate the working of the manufacturing concern. Under the globalize economy, mere planning is not enough. Efforts are constantly made to scrutinize the results of the workings. If so, out of control situations may be find out and eliminated immediately, with the help of cost control, the executives can limit the costs within the planned level.

Characteristics of Cost Control

The characteristics of cost control are presented below:

1. Delineation of Centers of Responsibility: Overlapping operations and responsibilities destroy the very essence of cost control.

2. Delegation of Authority: If persons are charged with responsibility without authority, the cost control will be ineffective. Hence, proper or adequate delegation of authority is necessary for proper cost control.

3. Measurement of Performance: A performance is to be measured with the help of reasonable criteria. Standard costing can be used as reasonable criteria. The person whose performance is being measured should participate in setting the standards.

4. Relevance of Controllable Cost: Only few costs are controllable at different levels of management. The management evaluates the performance of an employee with the help of costs incurred that are controllable.

5. Cost Reporting: Cost report provides a basis for effective cost control. Hence, if the cost reports is not prepared and submitted in time, the cost control cannot be exercised.

6. Constant Efforts: The measurement of performances, knowing functioning of manufacturing department and analysis of costs require constant efforts. This type of constant efforts leads to cost consciousness and result in cost control.

7. Policies and General Objectives: All the employees of the organization are communicated the policies and general objectives. If so, cost control is very easy.

Cost control is exercised through various techniques like standard costing, budgetary control, inventory control, quality control, performance analysis and reporting.

Steps Involved in Cost Control

The following steps have been adopted to exercise cost control:

1. Planning: Planning may be done as in the form of budget, standard, estimate and the like. The past events have been considered for proper planning. The planning is expressed both in physical as well as monetary terms. The standards are used as yardsticks.

2. Communication: The planning and policy should be communicated to the employees. If so, they can assume the responsibility and do the work properly. Communication has two directions. They are upward direction and downward direction. Instructions flow from the top level to lower level. Likewise, report on performance move towards upwards.

3. Motivation: The performance is evaluated; costs are ascertained and reported to the management regarding the results of performance. Such report may be act as motivating force and leads to better performance in the days to come.

4. Appraisals and Reporting: The actual performance is compared with preplanned standard and find the deviations. The causes for such deviations are also analyzed. Finally, the deviations with reasons are reported to the top level of management for cost control.

5. Decision Making: The top management may review the report on many directions. Lastly, the management takes necessary corrective actions. Finally, the existing standard or budget may be revised according to the prevailing situations.

The responsible executives can exercise physical control for the successful implementation of cost control system. In the manufacturing place, the supervisor can exercise control over the amount of expenditure incurred as in the form of cash or in the utilization of labour, material and other resources. If minimum materials are used, cost of material may be controlled to some extend.

Labour is employed on time rate basis. If so, maximum work can be completed within short spam of time. Thus, cost of labour is exercised. A machine is also used to produce a product. Increasing productivity may use minimum machine hours. In this way, the supervisor can exercise control in physical terms i.e. labour hours, machine hours and quantities of material, wastage and spoilage.

Advantages of Cost Control

The chief advantages of cost control are briefly explained below:

1. Return on capital employed may be increased.
2. The volume of profit is also increased with minimum output and sales.
3. Management can increase the productivity with available resources.
4. The employees are getting job continuously.
5. The employees can get reasonable remuneration with bonus.
6. The available factors of production and resources are effectively used.
7. The credit worthiness of the company is increased.
8. There is a possibility of prosperity and economic stability of the industry.

Inventory Valuation

Inventory generally refers to stock or stock in trade. In a trading concern, it refers to goods meant for resale or unsold goods. In a manufacturing concern, it includes items such as raw materials, semi-finished goods, and finished goods.

The Institute of Chartered Accountants of India (ICAI) defines in Accounting Standard 2 inventories as tangible properties held:

(a) For sale in the ordinary course of business, or

(b) In the process of production for such sale; or

(c) For consumption in the production of goods or services for sale, including maintenance supplies and consumables other than machinery parts.

The inventory valuation is done at the end of each financial year in order to assess the operating performance (i.e., to find out profit or loss) and the financial position of the business (along with others of the business through the balance sheet).

Generally inventory is valued at cost or market price, whichever is lower. The basis of stock valuation adopted should be consistent over a period in order to make comparative evaluation meaningful.

Objectives of Inventory Valuation

Determination of Trading Profit

Inventory is an important item for ascertaining the trading profit or gross profit. Gross profit is the excess of sales over cost of goods sold.

Cost of goods sold is computed by adjusting the opening and closing stocks to purchases, as shown follows:

Cost of goods sold = Opening stock + Purchases – Closing stock.

From the above equation it may be understood that the values of stocks influence the cost and thereby affect the gross profit. For example, over valuation of closing stock will reduce the cost and increase the current profit and reduce profits of subsequent years and vice versa.

Determination of Financial Position

Inventory plays an important role in the ascertainment of the financial position of a business. Closing stock is shown as a current asset in the balance sheet. Over and under valuation of stock will give a misleading picture about the working capital position and the overall financial position of the business.

Methods of Stocktaking

Stocktaking refers to the physical verification of the items of inventory in order to ascertain the value for accounting purposes.

Either one or combination of the following two methods can make the physical verification:

(a) Periodic Inventory System and

(b) Perpetual Inventory System.

Periodic Inventory

It refers to a system where stocktaking is usually done periodically; say once or twice in a year. It is actually done holding up purchases and sales for a day or two or a week. Under this method, the items of inventory are physically counted, weighed and verified thoroughly depending upon the nature of items. Then they are listed out in a Stock Sheet and priced and values ascertained.

Perpetual Inventory System

This is a method of recording store balances after every receipt and issue to facilitate regular checking and to obviate to close down for stocktaking. A programme of continuous stocktaking follows a perpetual inventory. Perpetual inventory means the system of records, whereas continuous stocktaking means the physical checking of those records with actual stock.

Under this method separate stock ledgers are prepared for each of the items of inventory e.g., stores ledger, work in progress ledger, finished goods ledger. The inventory purchases and issues are recorded in these ledgers on a continuous basis.

Hence, these ledgers show the balances of the respective items of inventory at any point of time. The physical verification is done on a continuous basis by comparing the physical balance with book balance. Discrepancies, if any, are located, investigated and necessary actions taken immediately. It is commonly used in large business concerns.

Valuation of Inventory

The method of inventory valuation is very important because it determines the amount of firm's investment in inventory and it influences the firm's reported income. In Financial accounting, the inventory is traditionally valued at lower of the cost or market value. On the other hand, in Cost accounting it is valued at cost of production.

Hence, the valuation of socks in two sets of books will be different and there will be difference in profits shown by financial and cost accounting records. This difference will be reconciled through a Reconciliation Statement.

Historical Cost

The actual cost of raw materials, Work in Progress, and Finished Goods is the most logical method of valuing inventory. Cost Accounting (Records) Rules also provide that the inventory should be valued 'at cost'. Historical cost of inventories is the expenditure incurred for bringing inventory in a saleable condition.

Accounting Standard 2 of the Institute of Chartered Accountants of India states that historical cost represents an appropriate combination of cost of purchase, cost of conversion, and other costs incurred in the normal course of business bringing the inventory up to the present location and condition.

Lower of the Cost or Market Price (LCM)

Under this method, the inventory is valued at cost or market price whichever is lower. The market price may be lower than the cost when the price levels of declining (during deflation) and the inventory may become obsolete because of technological and other changes, it is a conservative method. It shows a lower income than the income shown under the cost method.

However, when prices fluctuate, this method switches to period by period from cost to market price and vice versa. This reduces the usefulness of cost data for managerial analysis. It expects only losses but not gains.

Net Realizable Value Method

This method is used for inventories, which are damaged or partly obsolete. Net realizable value means the estimated selling price less cost of completion. Normally the stock is valued at historical cost as the selling price will be less.

The loss incurred by writing down the stock to the net realizable value is adjusted to the profit and loss account. The inventory value, under this method, should not exceed the expected realizable value.

Replacement Cost Method

Under this method, the inventories are valued at a price, which is equal to the current acquisition cost either by production or at a price that would have to be paid for those items at the inventory date. Or simply the replacement value may be taken as 'market value' or 'reproduction value'. This method is a conservative method since it takes into consideration all possible losses but not expected profits.

Hence, the inventory is valued at the minimum of:

(a) Historical cost;

(b) Replacement value; and

(c) Net realizable value.

This method is not approved by Income Tax Authorities. Similarly the accountants also do not follow this method in practice.

Example:

The following purchases and issues were made in a company:

1-8-2002	Purchases	300 units at Rs.15
6-8-2002	Issues	200 units
10-8-2002	Purchases	400 units at Rs.20
15-8-2002	Issues	450 units
22-8-2002	Purchases	400 units at Rs.25

What will be the value of stock on 22-8-2002 as per: FIFO

Solution: FIFO method.

Stores Ledger Account									
	Receipts			Issues			Balances		
Date	Qty.	Price $	Amount $	Qty.	Price $	Amount $	Qty.	Price $	Amount $
1-8-02	300	15	4,500	--	--	--	300	15	4,500
6-8-02	--	--	--	200	15	3,000	100	15	1,500
10-8-02	400	20	8,000	--	--	--	100	15	
							400	20	9,500
15-8-02	--	--	--	100	15	1,500			
				350	20	7,000	50	20	1,000
22-8-02	400	25	10,000	--	--	--	50	20	
							400	25	11,000

Value of Closing Inventory as on 22.8.2002 = $.11,000.

Job Costing

Job costing is usually a method of costing applied in industries, where the cost of the production is usually measured by the number of completed jobs. This is usually taken as a factor to measure the feasibility of jobs. These costs are recorded on a ledger throughout the whole job process and are added to the final balance statement when preparing for job costs and the batch statement.

Job costing method or system can be virtually used in any industry and is used to check whether if the cost of production exceeds the overheads and the price of the materials, so as to provide profit for the whole process.

Job costing is a technique of costing where the amount of work done is in the form of the number of jobs completed.

The production is taken with respect to the customer's orders and not as bulk for stocking purposes.

Moreover, the cost is not taken singularly but as a bulk of objects.

For example: Printing 5000 books, assembling 500 cars, delivering 4000 pamphlets and so on.

The elements within job costing procedure consist of direct costs, employment costs and material costs which comprises of prime costs and also overhead charges used for the departmental costs and shipping and handling costs which also includes costs taken for stocking and storage.

Documents used in a Job Costing System

1. Production order: Production order or cost order is a type of work order, authorising and sanctioning the manufacturers to produce, the order given to the customer. This process initiates the manufacturing process.
2. Cost sheet: For recording purposes, another type of document is present called the cost sheet. The cost sheet and the works order both can be combined at the last stage while establishing the final production value.
3. Other documents: The other documents are processed and submitted in between the manufacturing processes such as materials order, tool tickets, storage and stocking documents, warehousing, and inspection tickets.

Job Cost Accounting Procedure

The cost of the direct materials are taken calculated by the help of the materials requisition form. This is tallied by the accounts department. The employee wages are also calculated by taking the tickets issued by the payroll department. Moreover, if any over-head charges, these are also taken under consideration.

Manufacturing overheads are applied, at their respective departments during manufacturing. Then these are calculated together which constitutes the four main expenses of manufacturing. That is, direct expenses, direct labour, material expenses and manufacturing overheads within each department.

The job cost accounting procedures as a summary are given below:

1. Receiving an enquiry: Before placing the order, the customer usually studies about the manufacturer, what their rates are, what is the quality of the materials that they use, the time is usually taken by them to complete the order and so on.
2. Estimation of the price of the job: The cost of the job is done by the accountant keeping in mind the needs and taste of the customer. This includes the customer's preferences and choices. Another factor is that they also keep in track of the change in the cost of the materials, especially in recent years and specify the difference in cost. This job cost is then sent to the future customer.
3. Receiving of order: The customer will place the order if he is content with the job costs.
4. Production order: If the job is accepted, then a production order is given by the manufacturer within its subsidiaries. It is a form of authorised order which officially starts the production of the job. It is a set of instructions directed towards the foreman directing when and how the job should be done and how much should be completed in a day. Enough copies are made and passed throughout the departments so that each department can parallely keep in track of the jobs done.
5. Recording of costs: The costs are recorded and collected for each kind of job. For each department a certain job card is used, where the costs from different aspects of the jobs are taken into consideration.

These include:

Materials

1. Material requisition: Any document issued by the company stating the manufactures to transport the materials from the storage unit to the production house, so as to start manufacturing.
2. Bill of materials: A list detailing the materials, prices, components, sub-components for manufacturing the end product.

3. Materials issue analysis sheet: A form of document which consists of materials, their related details and when it was issued for the manufacturers.

Wages

1. Operation schedule: It is a form of the timetable which is related to the allocation and reissuing of resources in an organization.

2. Job card: A form of card used to detail about the details of the job needed to be done in a production facility. It instructs the foreman what to do as a set of instructions. Helpful for both the parties involved in the business.

3. Wages analysis sheet: It is a derivative of the income statement. It consists of the payroll statements and the wages for both the manufacturing and non-manufacturing employees depending on whether if it is a fixed salary or an hourly wage.

Overheads

Miscellaneous costs: These include hidden costs such as transportation, stocking, storage, food, infrastructure etc.

Completion of Job

On the completion of the job, a report stating the completion of the job is given to the accounts department where the final cost calculation takes place. The final cost statement is then compared with the estimated cost, to ensure whether it was a profit or loss.

Calculating the Profit or Loss

These costs are calculated when the final expenditure is compared with the estimated expenditure.

Objectives of Job Costing

1. To maintain the development of each job, by providing a separate account for each and every process of the job, so as to estimate the costs taken, when transitioning from one process to the another.

2. Helps the management in estimating the price of a certain work based on the price of the previous jobs.

3. To identify profitable and non-profitable jobs and help and prevent profitless jobs taking place.

4. To differentiate departments from one another on the basis of the cost taken and the amount of materials required.

5. Provide detailed information of what is happening in each department to the customer and move forward with the plan with respect to the idea of the customer. Any sudden changes in the plan can be accommodated, if congruent with the final cost estimation.
6. Job costing should be flexible and scalable enough to accommodate any kinds of industrial or commercial jobs available for cost estimation.

Features of Job Costing

According to Eric Kohler, "Job costing is a method of cost accounting whereby cost is compiled for a specific quantity of product, equipment, repair or other services that move through the production process as a continuously identifiable unit, applicable material, labour, direct expenses and usually a calculated portion of the overhead being charged to job order."

Some of the characteristics of the job costing process are:

1. Most of the manufacturing and non-manufacturing entities have acquired the job costing process.
2. The entities which have adopted job costing manufacture goods over customers demand and not for stocks.
3. In such entities, the total work is assessed into various jobs and also each job is appraised as a separate cost unit.
4. In this method, the production is not a continuous one.
5. An account is opened for the particular jobs including all the extra things, to know the exact cost of the job.
6. As every job is different, the procedure of job costing for it also differs.
7. The job of the cost is finalized after the job is completed.
8. The real-time profit or loss is decided, only after comparing the actual cost with the charged cost of the job.
9. Using job costing, the profit and each job's cost can be found out separately.

Here the organization does not have to spend on selling and distribution, the customers are responsible for placing orders and collecting the goods

Some of the Organization types which adopted job costing are:

1. Printers Machine tool manufacturing industries.

2. Interior decorations.
3. Advertising concerns.
4. Furniture making industry.
5. Musical instruments manufacturing industry.
6. Management consulting industry.
7. Toy making industry.
8. Engineering workshop.

Few objectives of costing: Now let us look at the advantages and disadvantages of cost accounting.

Advantages of Job Costing

1. Job costing acts as a form of analysis detailing all the type of costs that are present throughout the manufacturing process. This includes the direct costs, the labour costs, and the overhead charges.
2. It acts as a gauge determining the profitability of the job and helps for the future customers or companies to decide whether to take up the job or not. It also gives us an idea about the feasibility of the job.
3. Job costing prevents duplication of work because it helps in the estimation of a similar job. This helps in a company quoting the price of a job, it can always depend on the pricing of a previous job as a reference.
4. The efficiency of the manufacturers can also be taken into observation while taking account of their job costing and their associated expenses.
5. Ruination and defective work can be found out through job costings and it can be immediately corrected through certain individuals responsible for the job.
6. Budgetary control comes into action when taken consideration of the various overhead charges which are predetermined for each department.
7. Job costing information is used more for job contacts where the price of the job depends on the amount of the work done, rather than depending on the final fixed price.
8. It evaluates the quality of the work through various statistical techniques.
9. Job costing provides an easy calculation of cost overheads for specific needs, and in a precise manner.

10. Job costing enables the supervisors to keep track of various components such as money, materials and the performance of the employees.

Disadvantages of Job Order Costing

1. Based purely on costs. This method, is disadvantageous in fixing prices for the complete process, as the costs are recorded along each step. Hence it makes is difficult to prevent unwanted costs and expenditures occurred in between the processes.

2. It is very expensive because records are to be made for each and every step of the order. Starting from the materials list to the final product statement. Hence capital is needed to keep such records properly.

3. There is no exact procedure for estimating the job cost since there are no specific methods to differentiate direct and indirect costs occurring in a process.

4. This method of price estimation, may not be useful for jobs which are cost-efficient and fast-paced.

5. No standard procedure to follow while estimating. The only thing that can be followed is the need for supervision when calculating costs. So as to prevent any miscalculations and forgery of the prices and materials respectively.

6. More and more clerical work is required to detail about the measures and quota taken in each and every step of the project from the start to the finish.

7. Highly expensive because of the number of people working for a single project and unwanted expenditures may also be present.

8. No control of costs, since quality control and price control are usually done after the estimation of the final price. That too price control can also be done under a limit. Only to visible price variations, there is a chance of hidden costs that may not be recorded.

9. These kinds of jobs are only applicable, depending on the nature of the market and not on the nature of the job assigned. This becomes useless when the behaviour of the consumer market doesn't support such jobs, more and more expenditure for man, machine and materials takes place.

10. During inflation and recession, such jobs are useless and comparing such job costs are fruitless and a waste of time. Ordering job costs during the time of inflation is not considered smart.

11. No form of correction can take place if the actual profit is less than the estimated profit. The only thing we can do while calculating job costs is preventing loss to both the consumer and the manufacturer.

12. Since overheads are allocated to each department on a predetermined basis, there is no strict method to control the cost of the project using job costing.

13. Record keeping is what keeps the process of job costing alive. If there is no sufficient record work, then it can cause a huge downfall to the whole project and it may lead to a huge loss to the manufacturer.

14. There is no 100% accurate estimation of the total final cost of a job using job costing.

Job costing is an efficient method in keeping track of the expenditure against the given revenue, that is, the income or the fixed budget by the customer. It expands to all industrial professions and people of different designations.

Job costing depends on the type of work that is done, rather than being applicable to any kind of job. This way the result is suited to the customer's needs and choices.

Usually, job costings are done by contractors, architects and consultants. People who own a small convenience or a hardware store doesn't have to use job costing techniques. Using job costing helps you to focus on the strongest and the weakest link of the business.

Hence, it helps the manufacturers to focus on the strongest link to produce more and more profits while giving expert care to the weakest links, so as not to provide any unwanted losses.

References

- Capital-budgeting: edupristine.com, Retrieved 2 June, 2019
- What-is-capital-budgeting: accountingtools.com, Retrieved 14 January, 2019
- Capitalbudgeting: investopedia.com, Retrieved 7 March, 2019
- Understanding-cost-variability: assignmenthelp.net, Retrieved 17 July, 2019
- What-is-a-cost-variance: accountingcoach.com, Retrieved 19 May, 2019
- What-is-manufacturing-overhead-and-what-is-included: accountingcoach.com, Retrieved 8 February, 2019
- Cost-of-capital: xplaind.com, Retrieved 9 August, 2019
- Capacity-management-cost-accounting, overheads, cost-accounting: accountingnotes.net, Retrieved 12 January, 2019
- Cost-control-meaning-characteristics-steps-advantages: accountlearning.com, Retrieved 10 May, 2019
- Inventory-valuation-meaning-objectives-and-methods, inventory-valuation, cost-accounting: yourarticlelibrary.com, Retrieved 21 February, 2019
- Job-costing-meaning-objectives-advantages-disadvantages: wisestep.com, Retrieved 23 April, 2019

Cost Accounting System

The framework which is used by companies for estimating the cost of their products for the purpose of analyzing the profitability, cost control and inventory valuation is known as cost accounting system. This chapter has been carefully written to provide an easy understanding of the varied facets of cost accounting systems as well as their types, advantages and disadvantages.

A cost accounting system is used by manufacturers to record production activities using a perpetual inventory system. In other words, it's an accounting system designed for manufacturers that tracks the flow of inventory continually through the various stages of production.

A typical cost accounting system works by tracking raw materials as they go through the production stages and slowly turn into finished goods in real time. When the raw materials are put into production, the system immediately records the use of the materials by crediting the raw materials account and debiting the goods in process account. Since most products go through many stages before they can be called finished goods, there are often several different work in process accounts.

Example: As the materials move from one operation to the next, the cost accounting tracks the progress and updates it in the computerized system. This is extremely helpful for production managers and cost accountants, so they can see how much inventory is in every stage of production at any point in time.

It also allows companies to maintain just-in-time inventory systems where materials are only ordered from vendors and supplies on an as needed basis. No extra quantities are ordered and stored for processing at later point. The company only orders enough materials to fulfill the current customers' orders. This saves the company on many different costs including storage, security, and obsolescence.

Essentials of a Cost Accounting System

The essential features, which a good Cost Accounting System should possess, are as follows:

1. Cost Accounting System should be tailor-made, practical, simple and capable of meeting the requirements of a business concern.

2. The data to be used by the Cost Accounting System should be accurate; otherwise it may distort the output of the system.
3. Necessary cooperation and participation of executives from various departments of the concern is essential for developing a good system of Cost Accounting.
4. The Cost of installing and operating the system should justify the results.
5. The system of costing should not sacrifice the utility by introducing meticulous and unnecessary details.
6. A carefully phased programme should be prepared by using network analysis for the introduction of the system.
7. Management should have a faith in the Costing System and should also provide a helping hand for its development and success.

Types of Accounting Systems

The two common cost-accounting systems are job order costing and process costing. Each has a specific use and helps companies track production costs based on their manufacturing methods.

Job Order Costing

Set up the individual accounts to record production costs. Accounts include inventory, factory labor, manufacturing overhead, work in process, finished goods and cost of goods sold. The accounts are in the company's general ledger and follow its standard numbering system.

Use a perpetual inventory system to track inventory costs. Perpetual inventory systems update general ledger accounts for any movement of inventory. This system works best for job order costing, as the manufacturer may have multiple jobs working at one time.

Compute production costs per job. Job order costing requires the use of order sheets. This sheet lists the necessary materials and labor needed to produce the product. Accountants track these costs based on the report information.

Allocate manufacturing overhead using a predetermined overhead rate. This rate is the expected indirect costs for all jobs. An allocation factor such as labor hours allows a company to allocate only the portion of indirect costs used on specific jobs.

Process Costing

Set up the individual accounts to record production costs. Accounts include inventory, factory labor, manufacturing overhead, work in process, finished goods and cost of goods sold. The accounts are in the company's general ledger and follow its standard numbering system.

Identify the processes that will drive the production of goods. Processes may include mixing, refining, separating, finishing and packaging. Costs allocated to goods depend on the number of processes used to produce goods.

Implement a periodic inventory system to track materials. This system computes inventory based on the dollar cost used to produce a batch of product. Computed once a month, the formula adds purchases to beginning inventory and subtracts inventory used to determine final inventory.

Report production costs using a batch cost report. The information contained on the report lists all costs for a particular batch of produced goods.

Cost Accounting System for Internal Decision Makers

The cost accounting system approach is applicable to all kinds of business, whether it is manufacturing or trading products, or whether it is delivering services.

To better understand what a cost accounting system is, it is important to know the difference between fixed costs and variable costs. Fixed costs are that would be the same from one period to another regardless of the level of production. Examples of fixed costs are depreciation and the cost of departments like maintenance, tooling, production control, purchasing, quality control, storage and handling, plant supervision and engineering.

By contrast, variable costs are called such because they vary directly with the amount of production. For example, manpower cost would be variable, because the number of employees hired would depend on how much or how little production is anticipated.

Fixed costs gained increasing importance since the industrial revolution because it is this kind of costs that were used as basis for the pricing of a product or service.

Cost accounting system is very much different from a financial accounting system. Whereas the former deals with cost control and reduction, the latter is focused on the actual and projected results, or the items in the profit and loss statements. And whereas a cost accounting system guides executives and managers, all internal to the company, financial accounting is of more interest to government regulators, creditors, investors and the general public.

A cost accounting system requires five basic parts. These are an input measurement basis, an inventory valuation method, a cost accumulation method, a cost flow assumption, and a capability of recording inventory cost flows at particular intervals.

A cost accounting system is based on the type of costs flowing into and through the inventory accounts. There are three to choose from: pure historical costing, normal historical costing and standard costing.

Pure historical costs refer to the costs of direct labor, direct material and factory overhead that have been recorded. Normal historical costs refer to historical costs for direct material and direct labor costs but an overhead is charged or applied to the inventory through a pre-determined rate per activity measure. In a standard cost system, all manufacturing costs are applied, or charged to the inventory, using standard or predetermined prices and quantities.

Without a cost accounting system, a business may make decisions that would lead to profit loss. The objective of a cost accounting system is to lower the cost of the business operation through identifying and controlling them. thus, profits will be maximized.

Many different types of a cost accounting system are available for managers from all kinds of businesses and industries to choose from. The best way to choose is to ask which one best allocates costs incurred in order to produce goods. Some of these factors for consideration are the production volume, manufacturing complexity, the number or products or product lines, and changes in the production process. Weighing all these would enable the decision maker to identify which type of cost accounting system would best empower him or her to minimize costs and maximize profits.

Advantages of Cost Accounting System

A good system of cost accounting serves management in the following ways:

Classification and Sub-divisions of Costs

Costs are collected and classified by various ways in order to provide information to management for control purposes and to ascertain the profitability of each area of activity. It enables a concern to measure the efficiency, and then to maintain and improve it. Unprofitable activities are disclosed and steps can be taken to make an improvement in those activities.

Control of Materials, Labour and Overhead Costs

An efficient check is provided on stores and materials. Stores Ledger and Material Abstracts are maintained which provide an effective check on the stores and material used in a business. By adopting the maximum limit for stores the total capital outlay is controlled and total financial loss due to over-stocking is obviated. Information of stock of various materials and stores is constantly available.

This helps in planning the production according to availability of materials and fresh stocks can be arranged in time. Loss due to carelessness or pilferage or any other mischief is detected and steps may, therefore, be taken to minimise such loss in future. An efficient check on labour and machines is provided by giving detailed information about the availability of machine and labour capacity.

The work is so planned that no section is over-worked and no section remains idle. The maintenance of time and job cards for workers discloses the loss incurred by idle time and indicates the directions in which losses may be minimised. The relative advantages of remunerating labour on the time or piece work or premium plans may be ascertained. It also measures the efficiency of the wage system in use.

Cost Accounting thus provides a detailed control of materials and stores and labour costs. Various techniques of materials control are applied in order to avoid the excessive locking up of capital in stock of materials and stores. Idle time should be kept as low as possible. By having proper classification of overheads into controllable and uncontrollable or fixed and variable, it helps to control the overhead costs.

Business Policies

Business Policy may require the consideration of alternative methods and procedures and this is facilitated by cost information correctly presented. For example, by the aid of cost reports management can decide whether the manufacture of certain products increases overhead expenditure disproportionately or whether to treat by-products even at a loss to make possible a more important trade in another product.

Thus, it helps management to take vital decisions such as introduction of a new product, selection of a most profitable product mix, utilisation of spare capacity, exploration of additional market, whether to make or buy, problem of limiting factor, replacement of existing assets, appraisal of proposed investment to meet expansion programme etc. with the help of marginal costing techniques and differential cost analysis.

Budgeting

It provides the use of budgets and performance reports and enables management to correct inefficiencies before they enter into business. It is a coordinated plan of action for every responsible person for comparing the actual results with the budgets. Two important cost accounting tools for helping managers are budgets and performance reports. Budgets are financial and/or quantitative statements prepared and approved prior to a defined period of time, of the policies to be pursued during that period for the purpose of attaining objectives of management.

Thus, budgets are the formal quantifications of the plans of management. Performance reports measure actual performance and give accounts of comparisons of budgets with actual results which facilitate action against those persons whose performance is less than the performance specified in the budgets.

The technique of control through performance reports is technically known as management by exception, which is the practice of concentrating on areas whose performance is not upto the mark as it was planned and ignoring areas that are running smoothly as these were planned.

Standards for Measuring Efficiency

It provides the use of standards to assist management in making estimates and plans for future and to provide the basis of management of efficiency. Actual are compared with predetermined standards to determine the operating efficiency.

Best use of Limited Resources

In all varied fields we are concerned to make the best use of limited resources that are available to us. Thus the intention is to obtain the maximum output from a given input. Cost Accounting provides the reliable data of costs with regard to materials, wages and other expenses.

These help management to get maximum output at the minimum cost by indicating where economies may be affected, waste eliminated and efficiency increased ; some of the loss occasioned by reduced turnover and falling prices may be avoided.

Instrument of Management Control

It provides management with valuable data for planning, budgeting and control of costs. The organisation and management of undertaking must be planned and controlled in such a way that the desired volume of production is achieved at the least possible cost in relation to the scheduled quantity of the product.

The measurement of the degree to which this objective is attained, is provided by cost accounting.

Example of Cost Accounting System

As the materials move from one operation to the next, the cost accounting tracks the progress and updates it in the computerized system. This is extremely helpful for production managers and cost accountants, so they can see how much inventory is in every stage of production at any point in time.

It also allows companies to maintain just-in-time inventory systems where materials are only ordered from vendors and supplies on an as needed basis. No extra quantities are ordered and stored for processing at later point. The company only orders enough materials to fulfill the current customers' orders. This saves the company on many different costs including storage, security, and obsolescence.

The real time component of the system is its most valuable feature. Management can make decisions based on current data and don't have to wait for reports to be aggregated. Although important, this feature is not always easily achieved. Most companies either use a bar code system or implant each product with an RFID chip to track its location in the production process.

Manufacturers using job order cost accounting and process cost accounting can both benefit from cost accounting systems.

Advantages and Disadvantages

Advantages of Cost Accounting

The benefits of cost accounting include:

Adaptability

Managers appreciate cost accounting because it can be adapted, tinkered with, and implemented according to the changing needs of the business. Unlike static, Financial Accounting Standards Board (FASB)-driven financial accounting, cost accounting need only concern itself with internal eyes and internal purposes.

Ease of Monitoring and Controlling Labor Costs

Labor costs are easier to monitor and control through cost accounting. Depending on the nature of the business, wage expenses can be taken from orders, jobs, contracts, or departments and sub-departments. This means management can pick and choose how it determines efficiency and productivity. This is very important when estimating the marginal productivity of individual employees.

Ability to View Data in Different Ways

Cost accounting can be thought of as a sort of three-dimensional puzzle. Accounts, calculations, and reports can be manipulated and viewed from different angles. Management can analyze information based on criteria that it values, which guides how prices are set, resources are distributed, capital is raised, and risks are assumed. It's a crucial element in management discussion and analysis.

Disadvantages of Cost Accounting

Cost Accounting is not without Drawbacks:

Costs

The benefits of cost accounting come with a price. Since costing methods differ from organization to organization, it's not clear how these costs might manifest themselves until a specific firm is examined.

Complexity

Generally speaking, complex cost accounting systems require a lot of work on the front end, and constant adjustments need to be made for improvements.

Additional Steps to Verify Accuracy

Even if the rigidity of financial accounting creates some inherent disadvantages, it does remove the uncertainty and misapplication of accounting guidelines of cost accounting. Uncertainty equals risk, which always comes at a cost. This means additional—and often more vigorous—reconciliation to verify accuracy.

Reliance on Highly-skilled Talent

Higher-skilled accountants and auditors are likely to charge more for their services. Employees have to receive extra training and must sufficiently cooperate with data input. Non-cooperation can render ineffective an otherwise beautifully constructed system.

Cost-Volume-Profit Analysis

Cost-volume-profit (CVP) analysis is used to determine how changes in costs and volume affect a company's operating income and net income. In performing this analysis, there are several assumptions made, including:

- Sales price per unit is constant.
- Variable costs per unit are constant.
- Total fixed costs are constant.
- Everything produced is sold.
- Costs are only affected because activity changes.
- If a company sells more than one product, they are sold in the same mix.

VP analysis requires that all the company's costs, including manufacturing, selling, and administrative costs, be identified as variable or fixed.

Contribution Margin and Contribution Margin Ratio

Key calculations when using CVP analysis are the contribution margin and the contribution margin ratio. The contribution margin represents the amount of income or profit the company made before deducting its fixed costs. Said another way, it is the amount of sales dollars available to cover (or contribute to) fixed costs. When calculated as a ratio, it is the percent of sales dollars available to cover fixed costs. Once fixed costs are covered, the next dollar of sales results in the company having income.

The contribution margin is sales revenue minus all variable costs. It may be calculated using dollars or on a per unit basis. If The Three M's, Inc., has sales of $750,000 and total variable costs of $450,000, its contribution margin is $300,000. Assuming the company sold 250,000 units during the year, the per unit sales price is $3 and the total variable cost per unit is $1.80. The contribution margin per unit is $1.20. The contribution margin ratio is 40%. It can be calculated using either the contribution margin in dollars or the contribution margin per unit. To calculate the contribution margin ratio, the contribution margin is divided by the sales or revenues amount.

Contribution Margin

	$	Per unit
Sale	$750,000	$3.00
Variable Costs	450,000	1.80
Contribution Margin	300,000	$1.20

$$\text{Contribution Margin Ratio} = \frac{\text{Contribution Margin}}{\text{Sale}}$$

$$= \frac{\$300,000}{\$750,000} = 40\% = \frac{\$1.20}{\$3.00} = 40\%$$

Break-even Point

The break-even point represents the level of sales where net income equals zero. In other words, the point where sales revenue equals total variable costs plus total fixed costs, and contribution margin equals fixed costs. Using the previous information and given that the company has fixed costs of $300,000, the break-even income statement shows zero net income.

The Three M's, Inc. Break-Even Income Statement	
Revenues (250,000 units × $3)	$750,000

Variable Costs (250,000 units × $1.80)	450, 000
Contribution Margin	300,000
Fixed Costs	300,000
Net Income	$0

This income statement format is known as the contribution margin income statement and is used for internal reporting only.

The $1.80 per unit or $450,000 of variable costs represent all variable costs including costs classified as manufacturing costs, selling expenses, and administrative expenses. Similarly, the fixed costs represent total manufacturing, selling, and administrative fixed costs.

1. Break-even point in dollars. The break-even point in sales dollars of $750,000 is calculated by dividing total fixed costs of $300,000 by the contribution margin ratio of 40%.

$$\frac{\text{Break-Even}}{\text{Sale Dollars}} = \frac{\text{Total Fixed Costs}}{\text{Contribution Margin Ratio}} = \frac{\$300,000}{40\%} = \$750,000$$

Another way to calculate break-even sales dollars is to use the mathematical equation.

$$\text{Break-even Sales Dollars} = \text{Variable Costs} + \text{Fixed Costs}$$

In this equation, the variable costs are stated as a percent of sales. If a unit has a $3.00 selling price and variable costs of $1.80, variable costs as a percent of sales is 60% ($1.80 ÷ $3.00). Using fixed costs of $300,000, the break-even equation is shown below.

$$\text{Break-even Sales Dollars} = \text{Variable Costs} + \text{Fixed Costs}$$

$$X = 60\%X + \$300,000$$

$$X = .6X + \$300,000$$

OR

$$.4X = \$300,000$$

$$X = \frac{\$300,000}{.4}$$

$$X = \$750,000 \text{ Break-even Sales}$$

The last calculation using the mathematical equation is the same as the break-even sales formula using the fixed costs and the contribution margin ratio.

2. Break-even point in units: The break-even point in units of 250,000 is calculated by dividing fixed costs of $300,000 by contribution margin per unit of $1.20.

$$\frac{\text{Break-even}}{\text{Sale Units}} = \frac{\text{Total Fixed Costs}}{\text{Contribution margin per unit}} = \frac{\$300{,}000}{\$1.20} = 250{,}000 \text{ units}$$

The break-even point in units may also be calculated using the mathematical equation where "X" equals break-even units.

$$\text{Break-even Sale Units}$$

$$\text{Sales} = \text{Variable Costs} + \text{Fixed Costs}$$

$$\$3.00X = \$1.80X + \$300{,}000$$

$$X = \frac{\$3000{,}000}{\$1.20}$$

$$X = 250{,}000 \text{ Break-even units}$$

Again it should be noted that the last portion of the calculation using the mathematical equation is the same as the first calculation of break-even units that used the contribution margin per unit. Once the break-even point in units has been calculated, the break-even point in sales dollars may be calculated by multiplying the number of break-even units by the selling price per unit. This also works in reverse. If the break-even point in sales dollars is known, it can be divided by the selling price per unit to determine the break-even point in units.

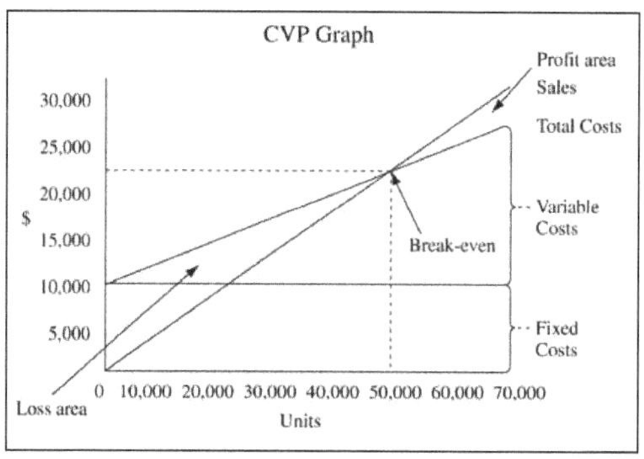

CVP analysis is also used when a company is trying to determine what level of sales is necessary to reach a specific level of income, also called targeted income. To calculate the required sales level, the targeted income is added to fixed costs, and the total is divided by the contribution margin ratio to determine required sales dollars, or the total is divided by contribution margin per unit to determine the required sales level in units.

$$\text{Required Sale in Dollars} = \frac{\text{Fixed Costs} + \text{Targeted Income}}{\text{Contribution Margin Ratio}}$$

$$\text{Required Sale in Units} = \frac{\text{Fixed Costs} + \text{Targeted Income}}{\text{Contribution Margin per Unit}}$$

Using the data from the previous example, what level of sales would be required if the company wanted $60,000 of income? The $60,000 of income required is called the targeted income. The required sales level is $900,000 and the required number of units is 300,000. Why is the answer $900,000 instead of $810,000 ($750,000 [break-even sales] plus $60,000)? Remember that there are additional variable costs incurred every time an additional unit is sold, and these costs reduce the extra revenues when calculating income.

$$\text{Required Sale in Dollars} = \frac{\$300{,}000 + \$60{,}000}{40\%} = \$900{,}000$$

$$\text{Required Sale in Units} = \frac{\$300{,}000 + \$60{,}000}{\$1.20} = 300{,}000 \text{ units}$$

This calculation of targeted income assumes it is being calculated for a division as it ignores income taxes. If a targeted net income (income after taxes) is being calculated, then income taxes would also be added to fixed costs along with targeted net income.

$$\text{Required Sale in Dollars} = \frac{\text{Fixed Costs+Targeted Income + Income Taxes}}{\text{Contribution Margin Ratio}}$$

$$\text{Required Sale in Units} = \frac{\text{Fixed Costs + Targeted Income + Income Taxes}}{\text{Contribution Margin Per Units}}$$

Assuming the company has a 40% income tax rate, its break-even point in sales is $1,000,000 and break-even point in units is 333,333. The amount of income taxes used in the calculation is $40,000 ([$60,000 net income ÷ (1 – .40 tax rate)] – $60,000).

$$\text{Required sale in Dollars} = \frac{\$300{,}000 + \$60{,}000 + \$40{,}000}{40\%} = \$1{,}000{,}000$$

$$\text{Required sale in Units} = \frac{\$300{,}000 + \$60{,}000 + \$40{,}000}{\$1.20} = 333{,}333 \text{ units}$$

A summarized contribution margin income statement can be used to prove these calculations.

The Three M's, Inc. Income Statement 20X0 Targeted Net Income	
Sales (333,333 * units x $3)	$1,000,000
Variable Costs (333,333 * units x $1.80)	600,000
Contribution Margin	400,000
Fixed Costs	300,000
Income before Taxes	100,000
Income Taxes (40%)	40,000
Net Income	$ 60,000

Benefits of Cost Volume Profit Analysis

Every organization needs to calculate future revenues in order to help the managers carry out their operations effectively. Cost volume is the approach used for this purpose. Cost Volume Profit analysis or CVP analysis helps in identifying the operating activity levels with a purpose to avoid any kind of losses and achieve profits. Moreover, it also helps the companies to plan their future operations and see whether their organizational performance is going on the right track or not. While conducting a business, the companies also have to face various risks and in order to counter those risks, CVP analysis is an effective tool.

Cost volume profit analysis can also help the organizations in calculating the breakeven point which is the point at which the profits become equal to zero. This can be done by finding the break even volume and then using it to make graphical representations. The break even volume can either be expressed in dollars or in units depending upon the nature and type of the organization. For instance: if the organization makes a large amounts of products, then the company must prefer to calculate the breakeven volume in the form of sales dollars while in case of one product company, the unit method might be a more effective calculation of sales volume. The calculation method and the graphical representation in both cases:

1. Break even volume in unit method = Fixed costs/Unit contribution margin.
2. Break even volume in sales dollar method = Fixed costs/Contribution margin ratio.

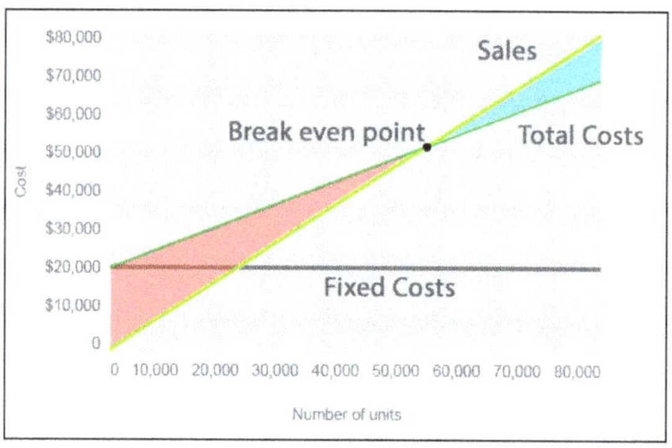

At the breakeven point, the profits of the company become zero and below this point, the company begins to incur losses. So, it is a beneficial tool for the organizations which help them to analyze what should be the target ad how this target can be achieved by managing the fixed as well as variable costs and also by preparing a plan for the future operations.

Benefits of Cost Volume Profit Analysis

Cost Volume Profit analysis helps organizations to examine their profits, costs and prices with respect to any changed that occur in sales volume. CVP is an effective tool that helps accountants to engage in decision making regarding future operations (Breakeven analysis). Moreover, it also helps in making the following decisions for the company:

- It helps to analyze which products and services are beneficial and how can company use these products and services to generate the maximum amount of revenue.
- It also explains what sales volume will be needed by the company in order to achieve a fixed level of profits.
- Moreover, it tells how much revenue should the company target so as to make sure that no losses occur.
- It also highlights what would be expected budget of the company.
- It also helps to calculate company's fixed costs and measure the amount of risk associated with any investment.

Operating Leverage

Another benefit that companies gain by using the CVP approach is the operating leverage benefit which explains how the cost structure of an organization is made up of fixed cost processes. This is a huge benefit because the cost structure is directly related to the level of growth and profit a company has.

Operating leverage can vary greatly from one company to another. In the firms that have a high ratio of fixed costs as compared to the variable costs, the operating leverage is good because it produces a high contribution margin. Similarly, higher fixed sales also mean that the company has a higher breakeven point. A higher breakeven point is directly related to the financial success of the company because at this point, the company can claim high profits at a much higher rate.

Income Tax Benefits

Similarly, the simple CVP model can be extended to other issues such as the calculation of incorporate taxes of multiple products within a company. This is done by modifying the profit equation of the chart to include taxes as well. This analysis can also be extended to those firms that offer more than one product or service rather than a simple product. This can be calculated as follows:

$$\text{After tax profit} = [(P-V)\,X - F] \times (1 - t)$$

Future Forecasting

Approaches and graphs, managers can analyze the direction in which their company is moving and this analysis might help them to better understand the different operations and activities within the organizations. By getting beforehand knowledge of profits and costs, the company can manage them in a more efficient way to increase productivity.

Preparation of Budgets

Since the cost profit volume analysis helps in determining the level of sales and thus helps organizations to achieve their desired targets. This approach would help the managers to prepare their budgets which consist of the costs as well as the revenues at any level of production within the organization.

Cost Control

The biggest benefit of CVP analysis is to evaluate the cost volume changes within an organization and the impact of these changes on revenue generation. For instance: there is a dental hospital that wants to purchase a new dental machine so that the patient's level of satisfaction can be increased by reducing the time required for dental treatment. The purchase of this new machine will tend to increase fixed costs of an organization. So, at such complex situations, the cost volume analysis can be the most effective tool to help in simplifying the company's decision. If this dental hospital uses CVP analysis, it can manage to decrease its variable costs by maintain the profit at the same desired level.

Price Determination

It is another benefit of using this approach. For example: If any competitor within the dental industry has set the price at $50,000 for a single dental operation and the business cannot provide this operation at any cost lower than $20,000, then the company can use cost profit volume analysis to compare the competitor's price with the fixed and variable costs of its own operations and thus it can manage to come up with a price that is in the best interest of the company.

Profit Planning

The aim of any business is to create value for the customers and to get profits for the company. However, managing all operations and costs in such a way that can maximize profits is not an easy task. Therefore, organizations have to consider a lot of things in order to engage in proper profit planning techniques. The CVP analysis can help the companies to create the best and most profitable combination of cost, price and sales volume. Thus, it can help managers to calculate and estimate their profit at different levels and for different range of products.

Risk Assessment

The business world is changing and due to several internal s well as external threats associated with any industry, businesses have to face too many risks. Although the calculation of risk and return through measuring a constant (beta) is a method in finance but managerial accounting is also concerned with this. Managing risk is too significant for any business because it tends to define all the procedures and practices involved within an organization.

Therefore, CVP is a tool which helps to calculate risk particularly in terms of costs and volumes. After analyzing this risk, the companies can come up with efficient solutions to reduce this risk.

Decision Making

Benefits of Cost Volume Profit Analysis directly or indirectly related to the decision making processes of a company. Any business organization has to make a lot of decisions regarding their price, their costs, and products, fixed and variable unit costs and so on. The CVP approach simplifies this process by providing the companies with a breakeven point and by helping them to engage in better decision making and planning for the future.

Cost Sheet

A statement, which is prepared at given intervals of time and provides information regarding the elements of cost incurred in production, is known as a Cost Sheet. It is a statement of various cost items extracted from the financial records or estimated on the basis of predetermined rate.

The cost sheet is generally prepared at short intervals and presents the total as well as cost per unit of products manufactured during the period. It is more or less like a Manufacturing Account. The difference is in the form of presentation.

A Production Statement or Cost Statement is a statement, which shows all the costs incurred, selling price of goods and profits earned during a period. In deed a production statement may be regarded as an expanded form of cost sheet. When it is drawn in the form of a T- account (the conventional form of account) it is called Production Account. Production account or Statement consists of two parts.

The first part shows the cost components and total cost of current production. The second part shows the cost of sales, selling price and the profit. The cost sheet can be drawn with as much details regarding costs as may be necessary.

Often, it includes cost data of previous year for comparison. Moreover, costs estimates can be prepared with the help of cost sheets and tenders for supply and price quotations can be submitted with greater reliability and precision.

Components of Cost Sheet

The components of total cost normally presented in a cost sheet are as follows:

1. Prime Cost: It is the aggregate of direct material cost, direct wages, and direct expenses.

2. Factory Cost: It includes prime cost plus all factories or works overheads. It is also known as works cost, production cost or manufacturing cost.

3. Cost of Production Or Production Cost: It is arrived at after adding office and administration overheads to factory cost.

4. Cost of Sales or Total Cost: It is arrived at after adding selling and distribution overheads to cost of production.

Table: Chart showing the components of total cost.

A. Direct Materials Direct Wages Direct Expenses	Prime Cost
B. Prime cost plus Factory Overheads	Factory or Works Cost (A)+(B)
C. Factory cost plus Office and Administration Overheads	Cost of Production (A)+(B)+(C)
D. Cost of Production plus Selling and Distribution Overheads	Cost of Sales or Total cost (A)+(B)+(C)+(D)
E. Total cost plus Profit	Selling Price

Items not Included in Cost Accounts:

Items of expenses, which are apportionment or appropriation of profits, should normally be excluded from costs. These are:

1. Income tax,
2. Dividends to shareholders,
3. Commission to partners, managing agents, etc.,
4. Capital losses,
5. Interest on capital (under certain circumstances),
6. Interest paid on debentures, and
7. Capital expenses, etc.

Treatment of Stocks

Stocks are generally of three types:

1. Raw Materials,
2. Work in Progress,
3. Finished Goods.

Stocks of Raw materials should be adjusted in order to arrive at the cost of consumption of raw materials.

> Raw Materials consumed = Opening stock of Raw Materials + Purchases less returns – Closing stock of Raw Materials

Work-in Progress is the value of semi- or partly finished goods at the time of preparation of cost sheet. The amount of work-in-progress should be adjusted to Factory Cost in order to arrive at Net Factory Cost.

> Net Factory Cost = Opening Work in Progress + Gross Factory Cost (i.e., Prime cost plus Factory Overheads) – Closing Work in Progress

Stocks of Finished goods should be adjusted to Cost of Production in order to arrive at the Cost of Goods sold.

> Cost of Goods sold = Opening stock of finished goods + Cost of Production – Closing stock of finished Goods

Advantages of Cost Sheet

1. It indicates the break-up of the total cost by elements, i.e. material, labour, overheads, etc.
2. It discloses the total cost and cost per unit of the units produced.
3. It facilitates comparison.
4. It helps the management in fixing selling prices.
5. It acts as a guide to the management and helps in formulating production policy.
6. It enables to keep control over cost of production.
7. It helps the management in submitting quotations or preparing estimates for tenders.
8. It is a simple and useful medium of communication of costs to various levels of management.

Specimen of a Cost Sheet

Cost Sheet for the period .... (Production .... Units).		
	Total Cost	**Cost per Unit**
	$	**$**
(1) Direct Materials: Opening Stock of raw materials Add: Purchases of raw materials Less: Closing stock of raw materials		
(2) Direct Labour		
(3) Direct Expenses		
(A) **Prime Cost**		
(4) Add: Works overheads or factory overheads		
(B) **Works or Factory Cost**		
(5) Add: Office and Administration overheads		
(C) **Cost of Production**		
(6) Add: Selling and Distribution overheads		
(D) **Total Cost or Cost of Sale**		

Items Required for Preparation of the Cost Sheet

1. Stock of Raw Materials

While preparing a cost sheet, it is necessary to determine the cost of raw material consumed.

If the opening stock of raw materials, purchase of raw materials during the period and closing stock of raw material at the end of the period are given, then the cost of raw materials consumed is calculated as follows:

Calculation of Raw Materials Consumed	
	$
Opening stock of raw materials	×××
Add: Purchases of raw materials	×××
	×××
Less: Closing stock of raw materials	×××
Cost of raw materials consumed	×××

2. Stock of Work-in-Progress

Work-in-progress refers to the semi-finished goods on which some work has been done but which are not yet complete at the end of the period. As such these goods are not yet available for state. The stock of work-in-progress may be valued at prime cost or factory/work cost basis, but generally, it is valued on the basis of work cost.

The adjustment for the stock of work-in-progress valued at works cost should be made as follows:

Adjustment of the Stock of Work-in-Progress	
	$
Prime cost	×××
Add: Factory overhead	×××
Add: Opening stock of work-in-progress	×××
	×××
Less: Closing stock of work-in-progress	×××
Factory or works cost	×××

3. Stock of Finished Goods

Stock of finished goods refers to the stock of products on which all factory work has been completed. Thus, it is valued at the cost of completed production.

If opening and closing stocks of finished goods are given, then the following adjustment should be made while calculating cost of goods sold:

Adjustment of the Stock of Finished Goods	
	$
Cost of production	×××
Add: Opening stock of finished goods	×××
	×××
Less: Closing stock of finished goods	×××
Cost of goods sold	×××

4. Carriage Inward or Carriage on Raw Materials Purchased

Carriage inward which is incurred on bringing the raw material purchased should be added while calculating the cost of raw materials consumed as below:

	$
Opening stock of raw materials	×××
Add: Purchases of raw materials	×××
Add: Carriage inward	×××
Less: Closing stock of raw materials	×××
Cost of raw materials consumed	×××

5. Scrap of Materials

Scrap is discarded material having some value which is usually either disposed off without further treatment or is introduced into the production process in the place of raw materials. If the value of scrap is negligible, then it is credited to profit and loss account as an income.

The cost of production bears the cost of scrap because total cost is not reduced by the amount of scrap. However, in case the value of scrap is significant, then it is deducted from the cost of material consumed or factory overhead/cost depending upon the stage of scrap.

If the scrap materials occur in raw condition stage, then the net amount realised from the sale of scrap should be deducted from the cost of materials used. But, if the scrap is obtained in the course of manufacturing process, then the net amount realised from the sale of scrap should be deducted from the factory overhead or factory cost.

6. Items Excluded from Costs

The items of expenses, losses or incomes which are related to capital assets, appropriation of profits, amortization of fictitious or intangible assets, abnormal gains and losses or items of purely financial nature do not form part of the costs and these are excluded from cost accounts.

The examples of such items include— loss on sale of building or machinery, interest on capital, discount on issue or redemption of shares or debentures, expenses relating to previous period, cash discounts, bad debts, damages payable, penalties and fines, interest or dividend received on investments, transfer fees received, profit on sale of fixed assets, appropriation of profits such as income-tax, dividend paid, transfer of profits to reserves or funds, donations and charities, excess provision for depreciation on fixed assets, amortization of fictitious or intangible assets such as goodwill written off, preliminary expenses written off, patents, trademarks and copyrights written off, capital issue expenses, underwriting commission, loss on issue of shares and debentures written off, etc. Thus, it should be noted that such items-are not taken into consideration (excluded) while preparing a cost sheet.

Illustration 1: From the following particulars of a manufacturing firm, prepare a statement of cost:

	$
Stock of materials on January 1,2011	20,000
Purchases of raw materials in January,2011	5,50,000
Stock of finished goods on January,1,2011	25,000
Productive wages	2,50,000
Finished goods sold	12,00,000
Works overhead charges	75,000
Office and general expenses	50,000
Stock of materials on 31st January,2011	70,000
Stock of finished goods on 31st January,2011	30,000
Selling and distribution expenses	3,00,000
Sale	12,00,000

Solution:

Statement of Cost

	$	$
Opening stock of raw. materials	20,000	5,00,000
Add: Purchases of raw materials	5,50,000	2,50,000
Less: Closing Stock of raw materials	5,70,000	7,50,000
Cost of raw materials used	70,000	75,000
Add: Productive wages		8,25,000
(a) Prime cost		50,000
Add: Works overhead charges		8,75,000
Works Cost or Factory Cost		25,000
Add: Office and general expenses		9,00,000
(c) Cost of Production		
Add: Opening stock of finished goods		
Less: Closing stock of finished goods		30,000
(d) Cost of goods sold		8,70,000
Add: Selling and distribution expenses		3,00,000
(e) Cost of sales		11,70,000
Profit		30,000
Sales		12,00,000

Illustration 2: The following extract of costing information related to commodity X for the half year ended 30th June, 2011:

	$
Stock on 1st January, 2011 :	22,000
Raw materials	17,600
Finished products (I ,600 tonnes)	
Stock on 30th June, 2011:	
Raw materials	24,464
Finished products (3,200 tonnes)	35,200
Purchase of raw materials	1,32,000
Direct wages	1,10,000
Rent, rates, insurance and works on cost	44,000
Carriage inward	1,584
Work-in-progress as on 1st January, 2011	5,280
Work-in-progress as on 30th June, 2011	17,600
Cost of factory supervision	8,800
Sales —Finished products	3,30,000

Advertising, discount allowed and selling cost 75 per ton sold. 25,600 tonnes of commodity was produced during the period.

You are required to ascertain:

a) The value of raw materials used,

b) Cost of output for the period,

c) Cost of turnover for the period,

d) Net profit for the period,

e) Net profit per tonne of the commodity sold.

Solution:

(Period : Six month ended 30th June ,2011)	(Output :25,600 tones)	
	$	$
Cost of raw materials consumed Opening stock Of raw materials Add : Purchase Of raw materials Add : Carriage inward	22000 13200 1584 1,55,584 24,464	

Less : Closing stock of raw-materials (a) Value of raw materials used Direct Wages Prime Cost Factory overheads :		1,31,120 1,10,000 2,41,120
Rent, rates, insurance and works on cost Cost of factory supervision Add: Work-in-progress as on 1st January, 2011 Less: Work-in-progress as on 30th June, 201 1	44,000 8,800	52,800 2,93,920 5,280 2,99,200 17,600 2,81,600
(b) Work cost (Cost of Output) Cost of output per tonne $= \frac{2,81.600}{25.600} =$ $ 11 per tonne		
Statement of Profit		
Works Cost (Cost of output)	Quantity (Tonnes)	Amount ($)
Add: Opening stock of finished products	25,600	2,81,600
Less Closing stock of finished products	1,600	17,600
Cost Of Goods Sold Selling and distribution overheads : Advertising. discount allowed and selling cost paise per tonne Of output sold for 24,000 tonnes.	27,200 3,200 24,000	2,99,200 35,200 2,64,000
(c) Cost Of Sales (Turnover) Sales		18,000 2,82,000
(d) Net Profit for the period (e) Net Profit per tonne of the commodity sold		3,30,000 48,000
$= \frac{48000}{24.000} =$ $ .2 Per tonne		

Benchmarking Costs

Benchmarking is a process where you evaluate various aspects of your operation in relation to the best practice for your business or industry. Regarding aviation operations, things that may be benchmarked relate to safety & operations, management, and costs.

For a safety benchmark, the lowest common denominator is the FAA (or other aviation authority) regulations. Those regulations don't really constitute a best practice, despite their often high level of requirements. A best-in-class type of benchmark here could be ISBAO (International Standard for Business Aviation Operation) certification. ISBAO seeks to establish the best practices for business aviation safety. Management benchmarking involves the "business" practices that can cover record keeping, training, communication and other areas related to running any organization. Benchmarks from various business schools can be adapted to your organization. Lastly, is costing. How does your aviation operation compare against a standard for costs.

A requirement of any benchmark is validity. Does it measure what it is supposed to measure? This is of vital importance. If certain costs are included or excluded, then you are comparing apples to oranges. Knowing what types of aircraft are obvious. as a small jet will see vastly different costs compared to a piston twin. Here are some less obvious areas to be careful.

Fuel costs. Sounds simple, however, what goes into that cost? What factors drive your cost per gallon? Operator A purchases fuel from its local FBO and pays $4.00 per gallon. Operator B has its own fuel farm and the cost of fuel is wholesale at $2.00 per gallon. However, the FBO includes the cost of running their fuel farm, taxes, and overhead. Operator B may look at their fuel farm cost as a facility cost and not allocate that in the per gallon cost. When we examine fuel costs, we look at all the costs that go into getting the fuel into the aircraft, including taxes, fees, and overhead.

Maintenance is a huge benchmark item and another hazard. What is included and excluded when comparing costs? An aircraft that just had a major inspection during the benchmark period will show significantly higher costs than one that didn't. In-house maintenance labor may be tracked and allocated very differently than that shown on the invoice from the service center. We tend to look at maintenance as if it were done at a service center - with itemized billing.

Part costs from a guaranteed maintenance plan are averaged over time while "pay as you go" part costs fluctuate over time. One unscheduled repair can drive up the part cost in any given period. You need to understand how long and what is included and excluded. For us, a basic part cost allocates routine scheduled and unscheduled part costs over their time interval.

Benchmarking other items such as hangar (lease, rent or own?), insurance (what liability limit?) and salaries (how many pilots, engineers, administrative staff?) all require knowing what is included in the respective cost categories.

Repeating a benchmark over time is needed to be able to measure trends. In any given year, there may be an abnormality in a benchmark item, so trends and long term data is always more useful. It is also helpful to be able to identify actionable items that can be taken to improve your operation. This may be pursuing fuel discounts, or reviewing the pros and cons of overhaul-exchange versus new parts purchases.

Benchmarking is a process for improvement, but you need to set it up correctly and understand just what it is you are benchmarking.

Benefits of Benchmarking

Companies from all different industries use benchmarking to gauge their successes and pinpoint their shortcomings. The general process of benchmarking involves identifying problem areas, selecting top competitors who excel where a company falls short and making the necessary changes. There are several key advantages to using benchmarking in an organization

Lowering Labor Costs

One advantage of benchmarking may be lower labor costs. For example, a small manufacturing company may study how a top competitor uses robots for several basic plant functions. These robots may help the competitor save a significant amount of money on labor costs. Company managers may obtain information on these robotics systems through the competitor's website or online articles. They may also identify the company that sold the competitor the robots. Subsequently, the company using benchmarking may call the robot manufacturer to help set up its own system.

Improving Product Quality

Companies may also use benchmarking to improve product quality. Engineers sometimes purchase leading competitors' products. They may then take them apart, study them and determine how the competitors' products outlast or outperform others in the industry. Chemical engineers may study food or cleaning products in a similar manner. They can then compare various elements contained in competitive products to their own product line. Subsequently, improvements can be made to product quality.

Increasing Sales and Profits

A company that uses benchmarking to improve its functions, operations, products and services may enjoy increases in sales and profits. Customers are likely to notice these improvements. The benchmarking company may also promote is improvements through company brochures, its sales reps, magazine and television ads. These efforts are likely to increase sales, especially among core customers. Companies that operate more efficiently due to benchmarking can drastically lower their expenses. These savings can be lead to greater profits.

Benchmarking across Departments

Some organizations use internal benchmarking to improve performance in different departments. Department managers may study and emulate the best practices of one particular department. These changes may spark improvements among all departments. Internal benchmarking has its limitations, however. The company's top department may not be functioning as efficiently as others in the industry. This means the other departments were not truly benchmarking against the best departments out there.

References

- Cost-accounting-system: myaccountingcourse.com, Retrieved 2 July, 2019
- Essentials-of-a-good-cost-accounting-system, cost-accounting: preservearticles.com, Retrieved 12 March, 2019
- Set-up-cost-accounting-system: bizfluent.com, Retrieved 22 January, 2019
- Cost-accounting-system: fasttrackph.com, Retrieved 3 May, 2019
- Advantages-of-good-cost-accounting-system, cost-accounting: yourarticlelibrary.com, Retrieved 19 August, 2019
- Cost-accounting-system: myaccountingcourse.com, Retrieved 9 February, 2019
- What-are-main-advantages-and-disadvantages-cost-accounting-method: investopedia.com, Retrieved 6 April, 2019
- Cost-volume-profit-analysis, cost-volume-profit-relationships, accounting-principles, accounting: cliffsnotes.com, Retrieved 29 January, 2019
- Benefits-of-cost-volume-profit-analysis, managerial-economics: mbaknol.com, Retrieved 17 April, 2019
- What-is-a-cost-sheet, cost-sheet, cost-accounting: yourarticlelibrary.com, Retrieved 9 June, 2019
- Cost-sheet-meaning-advantages-and-preparation, cost-sheet, cost-accounting: accountingnotes.net, Retrieved 18 February, 2019
- Articlesbenchmarkingcosts: conklindd.com, Retrieved 1 April, 2019
- Advantages-benchmarking-organization: smallbusiness.chron.com, Retrieved 7 May, 2019

Permissions

All chapters in this book are published with permission under the Creative Commons Attribution Share Alike License or equivalent. Every chapter published in this book has been scrutinized by our experts. Their significance has been extensively debated. The topics covered herein carry significant information for a comprehensive understanding. They may even be implemented as practical applications or may be referred to as a beginning point for further studies.

We would like to thank the editorial team for lending their expertise to make the book truly unique. They have played a crucial role in the development of this book. Without their invaluable contributions this book wouldn't have been possible. They have made vital efforts to compile up to date information on the varied aspects of this subject to make this book a valuable addition to the collection of many professionals and students.

This book was conceptualized with the vision of imparting up-to-date and integrated information in this field. To ensure the same, a matchless editorial board was set up. Every individual on the board went through rigorous rounds of assessment to prove their worth. After which they invested a large part of their time researching and compiling the most relevant data for our readers.

The editorial board has been involved in producing this book since its inception. They have spent rigorous hours researching and exploring the diverse topics which have resulted in the successful publishing of this book. They have passed on their knowledge of decades through this book. To expedite this challenging task, the publisher supported the team at every step. A small team of assistant editors was also appointed to further simplify the editing procedure and attain best results for the readers.

Apart from the editorial board, the designing team has also invested a significant amount of their time in understanding the subject and creating the most relevant covers. They scrutinized every image to scout for the most suitable representation of the subject and create an appropriate cover for the book.

The publishing team has been an ardent support to the editorial, designing and production team. Their endless efforts to recruit the best for this project, has resulted in the accomplishment of this book. They are a veteran in the field of academics and their pool of knowledge is as vast as their experience in printing. Their expertise and guidance has proved useful at every step. Their uncompromising quality standards have made this book an exceptional effort. Their encouragement from time to time has been an inspiration for everyone.

The publisher and the editorial board hope that this book will prove to be a valuable piece of knowledge for students, practitioners and scholars across the globe.

Index

CPSIA information can be obtained
at www.ICGtesting.com
Printed in the USA
LVHW060905030122
707669LV00002B/351

9 781647 260736